W9-DEV-975

THE
Tribeca Grill
COOKBOOK

THE *Tribeca Grill* COOKBOOK

CELEBRATING TEN YEARS OF TASTE

DON PINTABONA

WITH JUDITH CHOATE

PHOTOGRAPHS BY

SHIMON AND TAMMAR ROTHSTEIN

Copyright © 2000 by Don Pintabona

All photographs excluding those on pages xiii and xv copyright © 2000 by Shimon and Tammar Rothstein

Photographs on pages xiii and xv by Jeffrey Henson Scales

All rights reserved under International and Pan-American Copyright Conventions.
Published in the United States by Villard Books, a division of Random House, Inc., New York,
and simultaneously in Canada by Random House of Canada Limited, Toronto.

VILLARD BOOKS is a registered trademark of Random House, Inc.
Colophon is a trademark of Random House, Inc.

Library of Congress Cataloging-in-Publication Data
Pintabona, Don.
The Tribeca Grill cookbook/Don Pintabona;
photographs by Shimon and Tammar Rothstein.
p.   cm.
Includes index.
ISBN 0-375-50435-4
1. Cookery, American.
I. Tribeca Grill (Restaurant)   II. Title.
TX715 .P6573 2000   641.5'0974'1—dc21   00-026931

Villard Books website address: www.villard.com

Printed in U.S.A. on acid-free paper

2 4 6 8 9 7 5 3

First Edition

DESIGN AND ART DIRECTION BY JOEL AVIROM
DESIGN ASSISTANTS: JASON SNYDER AND MEGHAN DAY HEALEY

To the women who have nurtured me—
in their hearts,
in their kitchens—
Rosina, Nancy, and Christine Pintabona

In Memoriam
Robert De Niro, Sr.
You have surrounded us with the beauty of your art

WITH GRATITUDE AND APPRECIATION

AT THE RESTAURANT:

To our customers—many of you are now friends—for filling our tables with such warmth.

To our staff—both former and current—there would be no book
without your professionalism and loyalty.

To our investors—for giving us the opportunity—and to Bert Padell,
whose enthusiasm brought this illustrious group together.

To Bob De Niro—for your vision, passion, and trust.

To Drew Nieporent—for your confidence and pursuit of excellence.

To Jane Rosenthal—for your friendship and support.

To Ira Yohalem and Frank Franco—for keeping us balanced.

To Robin Chambers—for always lending a hand.

To the late Sybil Trent—for giving Drew the first fifty bucks to get started.

To Marty Shapiro—for managing to keep it all together.

To David Gordon—for sharing your tremendous wine knowledge, in the restaurant and in the book.

To Peter Klein—for making life at Tribeca always a party.

To Tracy Nieporent—for bringing laughter to our days.

To Agnes Chiao—for keeping us all in check.

To Josh Foster and all of our purveyors—for consistently providing us
with the amazing products we're able to work with.

To my former sous-chefs, banquet chefs, and pastry chefs—
all of you have contributed, in some part, to this book.

FOR THE BOOK:

To Judie Choate and Steve Pool—I think it's love.

To my agent, Mickey Choate—for finding the wheels that got us back on track.

To my editor, Pamela Cannon—for believing in our project.

To Joel Avirom—for putting your magical touch into the book.

To Tammar and Shimon Rothstein—for the great photos.

To Jimmy "New Shoes" Canora—you've come a long way from Ozone Park—
I couldn't have done it without you.

To Izabel Lam—for your exquisite plates.

To Bernardaud—for your beautiful china.

To my mentors, Georges Blanc, Charlie Palmer, Daniel Boulud, and Nishitani-san—you led the way.

And, certainly not least . . . my father, Carman—
for teaching me the values of hard work, loyalty, and dedication.
And my kids, Alex and Daniela—for keeping it fresh.

CONTENTS

PREFACE

WHEN I WAS ASKED TO WRITE a few words about the Grill, I didn't realize that more than ten years had passed since we first looked at the Martinson Coffee building.

In those years, many talented people have been involved in creating the Tribeca Grill, and Don is certainly one of them.

I'd like to express my appreciation to them, and most importantly to Don, without whom none of this would be possible. His consistency, talent, and loyalty have been unsurpassed.

Robert De Niro

FROM A RESTAURATEUR

OUR BEGINNING WAS VERY SIMPLE. As the owner of the three-star French restaurant Montrachet (established in Tribeca in 1985), I met Robert De Niro, who was one of our earliest guests. Although I was a great admirer of his work, we always respected his privacy and anonymity. One day, he looked up from his table and asked, "Would you like to do another restaurant in Tribeca?" Many claim that I responded with the *Taxi Driver* line—"Are you talkin' to me?" In truth, I was excited and intrigued.

Together, we walked to the abandoned Martinson Coffee warehouse on the corner of Greenwich and Franklin streets. What we saw was a special, dynamic space that, properly renovated, had enormous potential. It was our dream that it would become a world-class restaurant and film center. Robert De Niro deserves special credit for his vision and foresight in recognizing Tribeca's potential for rebirth and then acting upon it.

Tribeca Grill was developed as a partner for the Tribeca Film Center, which occupies the floors above it. It was planned that both the Film Center offices and the restaurant would retain much of the character of the once-industrial building. The concept was to create a restaurant space that appeared to have always been there—a simple and unpretentious gathering spot with exposed brick walls, warm wainscoting, windows that would fill the room with light, exposed beams and pipes, and, as the central draw, a huge, old-fashioned mahogany island bar (formerly the focal point of two greatly missed New York institutions, Jack Dempsey's and Maxwell's Plum), around which the restaurant would revolve. Tribeca Grill was created to serve as the dining room for the production companies located in the Film Center and the stars who visited and worked with them, to be a neighborhood watering hole for local artists, a meeting place for the mergers-and-acquisitions crowd from nearby Wall Street, as well as a destination point for Manhattan diners and visitors alike.

From the start, we were determined to create a restaurant with both the "sizzle" and the "steak." With celebrity investors like Bill Murray, Sean Penn, Mikhail

Baryshnikov, Christopher Walken, Ed Harris, Lou Diamond Phillips, Russell Simmons, Harvey and Bob Weinstein, Peter Max, Allen Grubman, Shep Gordon, Stewart Lane, Frank DiLeo, Paul Wallace, Meir Tepper, Robert Krasnow, David and Penny Trenk, Paul Yanowicz, and Joseph Eisenberg, we

Drew Nieporent (arms outstretched), Bob De Niro and the Tribeca Grill crew, circa 1990

had an immediate buzz. But we were ever mindful that "celebrity" and "trendy" restaurants could easily come and go. We decided to defy the odds and go for quality, substance, and longevity.

From the moment it opened, Tribeca Grill drew crowds. Obviously, at first, many came in hopes of dining next to their favorite actor. Although we knew that, initially, the food and service were not going to be the only lure, we prepared our menu and staff as though they would be. We all knew that, after the opening hurrahs, both critic and diner would judge us for just those two things. This determination has served us well as the restaurant has continued to gain worldwide recognition.

Hiring Don Pintabona as chef was a key decision to meeting this objective. Don was young, energetic, and well traveled. His journeys to Asia and Europe stimulated culinary ideas that gave the food as much of a "buzz" as our celebrity status. Together with our management team of Martin Shapiro, Peter Klein, David Gordon, Agnes Chiao, and Tracy Nieporent, we've all shared in a vision to provide a restaurant experience that is reliable, comfortable, and memorable.

Of course, since the Tribeca Grill remains as much renowned for its celebrity ownership and clientele as for its menu, a great deal of our cooking is done for public and private events. The restaurant has a separate Skylight Room for small private parties, a seventy-seat screening room, and a private dining room with its own catering kitchen plus the use of TriBakery next door for larger events. Most days and evenings, not only are we preparing the standard restaurant fare, but we also are executing the menu and details for one or more special events or private screenings.

For all of us at Tribeca Grill, it has been a labor of love and we would not trade our first ten years together for anything in the world. The passion that drives us is the same that lets us know the best is yet to come.

Drew Nieporent

INTRODUCTION

I came into the picture at Tribeca Grill in 1989, just days before leaving on my third trip to Asia. Two years had passed since my last stay in the Far East—working as sous-chef in a family-owned French restaurant in a small village between Osaka and Kyoto, Japan—and I was far more interested in returning to Asia than seeking a chef's job in New York. I was planning a six-week trip after completing a brief stint with Charlie Palmer (with whom I had also worked for two years at River Café in Brooklyn) at his new restaurant, Aureole, where I had first met Drew Nieporent and Robert De Niro. I was booked to fly out on a Friday when, early in the week, I was contacted by Drew, who wondered if I might be interested in a new project he was doing. "Sounds great," I said, "but I'm leaving in a couple of days. We'll have to talk quickly."

Drew promised to try to arrange a meeting with Robert De Niro for the following day. It took many, many telephone calls of confirmation and cancellation—"It's off. It's on. It'll be later. Can you do it now?" and so on—until, finally, I was scheduled to meet with Bob in a bar on Manhattan's Upper West Side. It was a terrible rainy afternoon and my mind wasn't really focused on getting a new job. But there I found myself, seated in the back of the bar, doing most of the talking. Nothing much about the restaurant business, mostly about traveling. Bob finally joined in the conversation when he realized that we had a mutual love of Asia. Quietly, De Niro asked if I had any questions for him. "Just one," I said. "Why do you want to do this? This is a crazy business. Lots of aggravation. The worst investment you could possibly make." Bob explained his plans for the Tribeca Film Center in a great old industrial building on Franklin Street with the bottom floor being earmarked for a comfortable, welcoming restaurant. "Fair enough," I said, and we parted without another word.

Afterward, I went off to meet up with a friend who lived in the area. When I called, he said, "Come on up. I'm just going out to pick up some eats and rent a video." "Rent a De Niro flick," I responded. "I'll explain." Since I had spent so much time out of the country, I really wasn't up-to-date on movies so I thought it might be a good idea to see a couple of De Niro's films. As luck would have it, my friend rented *Midnight Run.* Toward the end of the film, there's a scene with De Niro and Charles Grodin on a train. De Niro is doing some figuring on a piece of paper. Grodin says, "What are you doing?" De Niro answers, "Well, ya know, I was thinking, after I turn your ass in and collect my money, I'm gonna open up a nice little coffee shop." "Well, I have to tell you," Grodin responds, "a restaurant is a very tricky investment. More than half of them go under in the first six months. If I was your accountant, I would have to strongly advise you against it." It was almost, verbatim, my earlier statements. I thought to myself, "There goes that job. De Niro probably thinks I'm some sort of movie nut reciting his own movie lines back to him." But as destiny would have it, I was hired on Thursday and confidently left for Bangkok on Friday. For the first time in my life, I'd packed my bags knowing that I had a job to return to.

Once aboard, I told Drew that I wouldn't return until the restaurant was absolutely, completely ready to open (knowing well that nothing, in the New York restaurant scene, opens on schedule). What I didn't know was that, due to delays, I would spend seven months in Asia traveling through Burma, Thailand, Indonesia, and Malaysia. When the call came, I was more than ready.

I had spent years working just until I had saved enough money to take yet another trip to experience the food and culture of one more part of the world. Throughout my travels I had the opportunity to absorb the cuisines of over thirty countries. I really was ready to settle down for a while to develop menus incorporating the exotic flavors and ingredients discovered during my travels into the classic dishes that I had been taught at the Culinary Institute of America and in France under Georges Blanc and the Italian peasant meals that were my heritage.

I think it was the versatility of my experiences that made me a good match for the planned Tribeca restaurant. The Tribeca Film Center building was a hotbed of creativity: Miramax Films was establishing its mark in quality filmmaking, and

Tribeca Productions was emerging as an acclaimed production company. Bob De Niro was at the pinnacle of his profession, Drew was a rapidly rising star in the restaurant business, and together they wanted a chef with solid restaurant experience and a broad horizon of cultural influences whose culinary star had not yet risen. (I had spent so much time living outside the United States that I didn't know that chefs could achieve stardom.)

As I planned the menu for the "Grill," I tried to keep it straightforward and unfussy so that it would have a very broad appeal. I worked with familiar foods but gave many of them a twist. Gazpacho had its customary zesty raw vegetable flavor but it was embellished with chunks of sweet lobster meat (see page 78); fish might be simply grilled, but rather than a slice of lemon to emphasize its freshness, I would offer a Chili-Citrus Vinaigrette and Boniato Puree (see page 138); mashed potatoes became Peanut-Whipped Potatoes (see page 183); instead of spaghetti, I would use strozzapreti or other less-familiar pasta shapes with a simple fresh tomato sauce finished with some shavings of pecorino cheese. Diners came expecting a steak and a baked potato and were surprised at the quality and presentation of the food. This "surprise" has continued to give an extra sense of value and reward. Comfort foods in a comfortable setting have kept the kitchen humming with hundreds of meals daily.

Because so much of my cooking is for large numbers of people, it is extremely home-cook friendly. Much can be done in advance of service and many of the once-exotic ingredients that I frequently use are now easily found in supermarkets. In fact, I am often amazed at the bounty in the markets I visit throughout the country. Lemongrass, all kinds of herbs, a variety of chiles, Asian and Latin fruits and vegetables, are abundant. And you will find gourmet aisles laden with rices, flours, condiments, and ethnic foods that once would have been unthinkable at my dad's grocery store. Even with the possibility that you can't find everything you need at the corner store, mail order, Internet shopping, and FedEx will have the most exotic item at your doorstep overnight.

As Tribeca Grill celebrates its tenth year, I am often struck by how quickly the time has passed. For me, the one-time cook-and-run chef, this long period at one stove in my hometown has been remarkable. It has worked because the restaurant is the perfect blend of regular, local customers, stargazing tourists, celebrities, and power brokers; and because, over the years, I have been blessed with the confidence of Bob and Drew and teamwork from top-rate sous-, banquet, and pastry chefs, hungry young cooks, and a very loyal and hardworking support staff. Together, we have done what we set out to do—create a celebrity-owned restaurant that was casual yet upscale, with none of the pretension usually associated with a star turn. Plus, when one of the distinguished investors sticks his head (or hand) in the kitchen, the often-routine life of a cook gets just a little bit more exciting.

When I look back to my early years in the kitchen, when my grandmother told me stories of our Sicilian heritage as I watched her cook, I realize just how much I learned from her. As she cooked, she adapted the traditions of her homeland to the ingredients and recipes familiar to her now-American family. This practical inventiveness has served me well as I have incorporated the foods of the world to the demands of a high-profile restaurant kitchen, creating menus that were both recognizable and original. As I continue to travel, seeking new destinations with each trip, I have the opportunity to build a global culinary network with Tribeca Grill at the crossroads of my never-ending adventures.

Don Pintabona

THE

Tribeca Grill

COOKBOOK

Hors d'Oeuvres

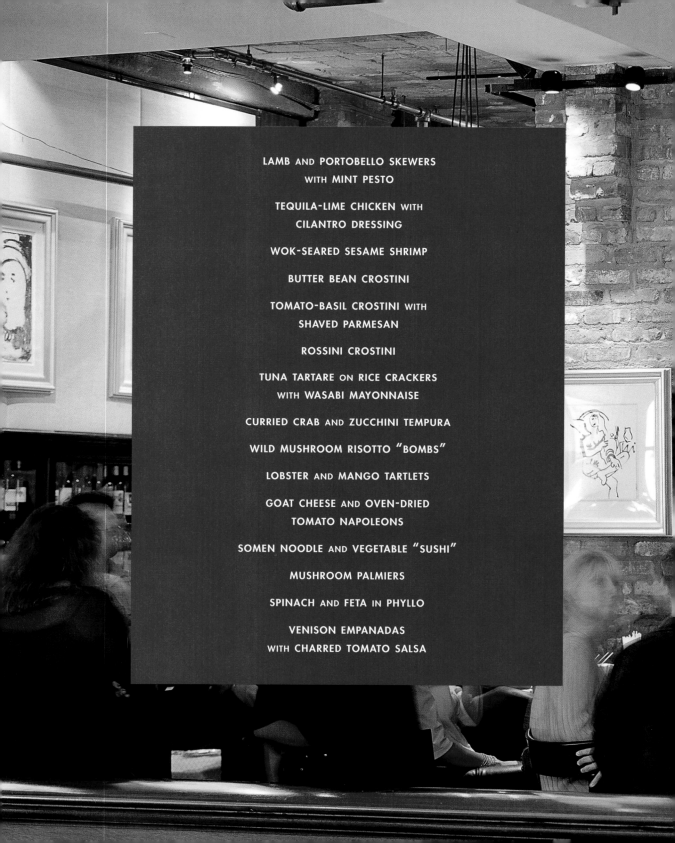

LAMB AND PORTOBELLO SKEWERS
WITH MINT PESTO

TEQUILA-LIME CHICKEN WITH
CILANTRO DRESSING

WOK-SEARED SESAME SHRIMP

BUTTER BEAN CROSTINI

TOMATO-BASIL CROSTINI WITH
SHAVED PARMESAN

ROSSINI CROSTINI

TUNA TARTARE ON RICE CRACKERS
WITH WASABI MAYONNAISE

CURRIED CRAB AND ZUCCHINI TEMPURA

WILD MUSHROOM RISOTTO "BOMBS"

LOBSTER AND MANGO TARTLETS

GOAT CHEESE AND OVEN-DRIED
TOMATO NAPOLEONS

SOMEN NOODLE AND VEGETABLE "SUSHI"

MUSHROOM PALMIERS

SPINACH AND FETA IN PHYLLO

VENISON EMPANADAS
WITH CHARRED TOMATO SALSA

LAMB AND PORTOBELLO SKEWERS WITH MINT PESTO

MAKES 30 SKEWERS

1 large bunch of fresh mint
¼ cup freshly grated Parmesan cheese
¼ cup toasted pine nuts
2 cloves garlic, peeled
Zest of 1 medium orange
¾ cup canola oil
Coarse salt and freshly ground pepper to taste
3 large portobello mushrooms, brushed clean
¼ cup olive oil
1 tablespoon minced garlic
1½ pounds loin of lamb, trimmed of all fat and silver skin

1. If using wooden skewers, soak 30 as directed on page 6.

2. Pick the leaves from the mint and quickly dip them in a saucepan of rapidly boiling salted water for no more than 3 seconds to blanch and set the color. Immediately drain and refresh under cold running water. Drain very well and pat dry.

3. Place the blanched mint leaves in a blender along with the cheese, pine nuts, garlic cloves, and orange zest. Pulse to combine. With the motor running, slowly add the canola oil, blending until the oil has emulsified into the mixture and the pesto is bright green and thick. Season to taste with salt and pepper. Remove from the blender and set aside.

4. Preheat the oven to 375°F.

5. Remove the stems and, using a small, sharp knife, scrape the gills from the mushrooms. Combine the olive oil and minced garlic and, using a pastry

brush, generously coat the mushrooms with the seasoned oil. Place them in a shallow baking dish and roast for about 25 minutes or until the mushrooms are tender and nicely browned. Remove from the oven and allow to rest until cool enough to handle; then slice, on the bias, into 30 strips about ⅛ inch thick and 2 inches long.

6. Using a very sharp knife, slice the lamb into 30 strips about ¼ inch thick and 2 inches long. (You will probably have some lamb left over.) Lay a mushroom strip on top of a lamb strip and thread the skewer through the 2 pieces. Continue making skewers until you have prepared 30. Season to taste with salt and pepper.

7. Place a large griddle, heavy-duty grill pan, or nonstick sauté pan over high heat. When very hot but not smoking, add the skewers, a few at a time, and sear for about 1 minute per side or until the outside is nicely browned but the meat remains medium-rare. Serve immediately with Mint Pesto on the side.

NOTE: The pesto can be made up to 24 hours in advance and stored, tightly covered and refrigerated.

The skewers can be put together early in the day and stored, covered and refrigerated. Season with salt and pepper and sear just before serving.

For attractive service, place a small bowl of the Mint Pesto in the center of a large round platter (which can be layered with fresh mint leaves) and lay the skewers in a wheel shape around the bowl.

Leftover pesto can be used as a dressing for pastas or pasta salads or as a condiment for grilled fish, chicken, pork, or vegetables.

CLOCKWISE FROM TOP:
Lamb and Portobello Skewers with Mint Pesto, Tequila-Lime Chicken with Cilantro Dressing, Wok-Seared Sesame Shrimp

TEQUILA-LIME CHICKEN WITH CILANTRO DRESSING

MAKES 30 SKEWERS

¾ cup tequila
¼ cup white wine vinegar
Juice of 3 limes
½ cup Lemon Oil (see Note)
5 large shallots, peeled and chopped
1 cup chopped fresh cilantro plus 1 large bunch of cilantro, leaves only
2 teaspoons minced garlic
1½ pounds boneless chicken breasts, trimmed of all fat
Coarse salt and freshly ground pepper to taste
½ cup canola oil

1. If using wooden skewers, soak 30 as directed on page 6.

2. In a small nonreactive container, combine ½ cup of the tequila with the vinegar and lime juice. Whisk in the Lemon Oil. When well emulsified, stir in the shallots, chopped cilantro, and 1 teaspoon of the minced garlic. Pour into a nonreactive, shallow container large enough to hold the prepared skewers. Set aside.

3. Using a very sharp knife, slice the chicken into 30 strips about ¼ inch thick and 2 inches long. Thread the strips onto the soaked skewers and place them into the marinade, leaving as much of the skewer exposed as possible as you do not want the wood to soak up the marinade. Cover and marinate for 8 hours.

4. Place the cilantro leaves in a saucepan of rapidly boiling salted water for 10 seconds to blanch and set the color. Immediately drain and refresh under cold running water. Drain very well and pat dry.

5. Place the blanched cilantro in a blender with the remaining ¼ cup of tequila and 1 teaspoon of garlic. Pulse to combine. With the motor running, slowly add the canola oil, processing until mixture is thick and bright green. Taste and adjust the seasoning with salt and pepper.

6. When ready to serve, remove the skewers from the marinade. Place a stovetop griddle, heavy-duty grill pan, or nonstick sauté pan over high heat. When very hot but not smoking, add the skewers, a few at a time, and sear for 1½ to 2 minutes per side or until the chicken is nicely browned and cooked through. Serve immediately with the Cilantro Dressing on the side.

NOTE: In the restaurant, rather than discarding juiced lemons, we use them to season oil. If you want to do this at home, combine 2 cups of vegetable oil with the shells of 4 lemons that have already been juiced and a few sprigs of fresh thyme in a heavy saucepan. Place the pan over medium-high heat and bring to a boil. Immediately lower the heat and barely simmer for 15 minutes. Remove from the heat and allow to cool. Strain into a clean container. Cover and store in a cool spot for up to 6 months. Use the oil for sautéing, frying, or for vinaigrettes.

The chicken may be marinated overnight and the skewers may be put together early in the day and stored, covered and refrigerated. Cook just before serving.

The Cilantro Dressing may be made up to 24 hours in advance and stored, tightly covered and refrigerated.

If desired, you can add a fresh cilantro leaf and a tiny wedge of lime to each skewer for garnish. You can also serve them as directed for the lamb skewers, replacing the mint leaves with cilantro leaves (see page 6) or you can cover a platter with coarse salt and stick the skewer ends into lime halves placed into the salt with the salsa served in a clear glass or attractive ceramic bowl placed in the center of the platter.

WOK-SEARED SESAME SHRIMP

MAKES 30 PIECES

1 cup sugar
½ cup plus 2 tablespoons cold water
1 cup Chicken Stock (see page 229)
¾ cup low-sodium soy sauce
¾ cup pineapple juice
2 cups plus 1 tablespoon cornstarch
Approximately 8 cups vegetable oil for frying
1 pound rock shrimp, well cleaned, rinsed, and patted dry
3 tablespoons sesame oil
1 tablespoon minced fresh ginger
1 teaspoon minced garlic
1 jalapeño chile, or to taste, seeded and minced
½ cup julienned scallion, white part only
2 tablespoons black sesame seeds (see Note)

1. Combine the sugar and ½ cup cold water in a heavy-bottomed saucepan over high heat and bring to a boil. Immediately lower the heat and gently simmer for about 20 minutes or until the liquid becomes golden brown as the sugar caramelizes. Stir in the stock and raise the heat to medium and simmer for about 15 minutes or until the liquid is reduced by one half. Add the soy sauce and pineapple juice and bring to a boil. Lower the heat and simmer for 10 minutes or until the liquid is reduced by one quarter.

2. Dissolve 1 tablespoon of the cornstarch in 2 tablespoons of cold water and whisk it into the reduced liquid. Bring to a simmer, whisking constantly. Simmer for about 3 minutes or until the teriyaki sauce mixture is silken and almost syrupy. Remove from the heat and set aside (see Note).

3. Line a baking sheet with paper towel and set aside.

4. Place the oil in a deep-fat fryer or deep saucepan over medium-high heat and bring to 365°F on a candy thermometer.

5. While the oil is heating, prepare the shrimp for frying. Place the remaining cornstarch in a plastic bag. Working with one quarter of the shrimp at a time, lightly coat them with cornstarch by placing them in the bag and shaking it. Shake off excess cornstarch and place the coated shrimp on a platter.

6. In batches, place the coated shrimp into the hot oil and fry for about 40 seconds or until the shrimp are golden and crispy. Using a slotted spoon, lift the shrimp from the oil and place them on the towel-lined baking sheet to drain. Continue frying until all the shrimp are cooked.

7. Heat the sesame oil in a wok over high heat. Add the ginger and garlic and sauté for 30 seconds. Add the chile and sauté for about 1 minute or until the mixture is very fragrant. Add the fried shrimp and toss to combine. Add ¼ cup of the reserved teriyaki sauce and gently toss just until the pan liquid is syrupy. Immediately remove from the heat and toss in the scallion and sesame seeds to lightly coat the shrimp. Serve immediately, using toothpicks as skewers.

NOTE: Small shrimp or scallops may be substituted for the rock shrimp.

Black sesame seeds are available from Asian and East Indian or Pakistani markets, specialty food stores, and some supermarkets.

The teriyaki sauce makes about 2 cups, of which you will only use one quarter. However, it stores well, covered and refrigerated, and will perk up a simple piece of grilled chicken, pork, or fish or add zest to some stir-fried vegetables and/or noodles.

Butter Bean Crostini

30 Crostini
One 16-ounce can butter beans or other rich white beans
*   such as cannellini, drained*
¼ cup finely chopped fresh flat-leaf parsley leaves
¼ cup olive oil
1 tablespoon fresh lemon juice
2 tablespoons minced garlic
Coarse salt and freshly ground pepper to taste

1. To make crostini, you will need ¼-inch-thick slices of baguette or ¼-inch-thick by 2-inch round pieces of peasant bread. For 30 pieces, combine ¼ cup olive oil with 1 tablespoon minced garlic and, using a pastry brush, lightly coat both sides of each piece of bread with the mixture. Season lightly with salt and pepper. Place the seasoned bread slices on a baking sheet with sides in a preheated 325°F oven for 4 minutes; then turn and toast the remaining side for 4 minutes or until golden. Remove from the oven and cool on a wire rack. Although you can make crostini a few days ahead of use and store them, uncovered, at room temperature, so they retain their crispness, they taste best made on the day they will be used.

2. Place the beans in the bowl of a food processor fitted with the metal blade. Add 2 tablespoons of the parsley along with the olive oil, lemon juice, and garlic and process until smooth. Taste and adjust the seasoning with salt and pepper. (If the mixture is stiff rather than thick and creamy, add a tablespoon or two of chicken or vegetable broth or even a little water to thin it.)

3. Spoon the butter bean puree onto the Crostini. Sprinkle with a bit of the remaining parsley and serve.

NOTE: You can also garnish the top with a single parsley leaf, a few whole beans, cracked black pepper, or a bit of finely diced raw or Roasted Red Peppers (see page 238).

TOMATO-BASIL CROSTINI WITH SHAVED PARMESAN

MAKES 30 PIECES

30 Crostini (see page 12)
½ pint each red and yellow pear tomatoes, well washed and halved,
*   or 10 ripe plum tomatoes, peeled, cored, seeded, and finely diced*
¼ cup finely diced shallots
¼ cup basil chiffonade (see Note)
¼ cup olive oil
3 tablespoons balsamic vinegar (see Note)
Coarse salt and freshly ground pepper to taste
¼-pound piece Parmesan cheese

1. Combine the tomatoes, shallots, and basil in a nonreactive mixing bowl. Add the olive oil and vinegar (see Note) and toss to combine. Season to taste with salt and pepper and allow to marinate for at least 30 minutes (or up to 8 hours).

2. When ready to serve, spoon about 1 tablespoon of the tomato mixture over the top of each Crostino. Using a cheese shaver (or box grater), shave a piece of Parmesan cheese over the top of each Crostino and serve.

NOTE: We use pear tomatoes because of their firm flesh, but any other tomato can stand in for them. The ripeness of the tomatoes is far more important than the type. You really need the summer-sweet taste of a perfectly ripe tomato to balance the acidic vinegar and the pungent basil.

"Chiffonade" is the French culinary term for thin strips of leafy greens (such as lettuces, sorrel, herbs). Chiffonade is simple to make by rolling up a bunch of well-washed leaves, cigar-fashion, and slicing them, crosswise, into thin pieces. Pull the cigar apart and fluff the strips. Herb or baby spinach chiffonade makes an attractive garnish for all types of hors d'oeuvres.

ROSSINI CROSTINI

MAKES 30 PIECES

30 Crostini (see page 12)
1 cup port wine
¼ cup balsamic vinegar
1 pound mushrooms, trimmed and brushed clean
2 shallots, peeled and chopped
2 tablespoons minced garlic
¼ cup olive oil
Coarse salt and freshly ground pepper to taste
1 pound foie gras, trimmed into an even square shape (see Note)
1-pound piece beef tenderloin, trimmed of all fat and silver skin

1. Preheat the oven to 350°F.

2. Combine the wine and vinegar in a small nonreactive saucepan over medium heat. Bring to a boil; lower the heat and barely simmer for about 20 to 30 minutes or until the liquid has reduced and the mixture is thick and syrupy. Remove from the heat and allow to cool.

3. Combine the mushrooms, shallots, and garlic on a baking sheet with sides. Drizzle the olive oil over the top and season to taste with salt and pepper. Toss to combine. Place in the preheated oven and bake for 25 minutes or until all of the liquid has evaporated and the mushrooms are nicely browned. Remove from the oven and place the mixture in the bowl of a food processor fitted with the metal blade. Process, using quick off and on turns, until the mushrooms are finely chopped but not pureed. Scrape the mixture into a clean bowl and allow to cool.

4. Place two nonstick sauté pans over medium-high heat. Season the foie gras and beef with salt and pepper to taste and, when the pans are very hot but not smoking, place the foie gras in one pan and the beef in the other. Sear the foie gras for 1½ minutes per side or until nicely browned and just about cooked through. Remove the foie gras from the pan and drain on a double layer of paper towel for at least 3 minutes before slicing. Sear the beef for 2 minutes; turn and sear the remaining side for 2 minutes or until an instant-read thermometer inserted into the thickest part reads 140°F. (If the beef sticks, add a bit of foie gras fat to the pan.) Remove the beef from the pan and allow it to rest for about 2 minutes before slicing.

5. Spread the mushroom mixture over each Crostino.

6. Slice the foie gras and the beef into ⅛-inch-thick slices. Place a slice of foie gras topped with a slice of beef on each Crostino. Drizzle the beef with a bit of the reserved port wine reduction and serve immediately.

NOTE: Fresh foie gras is available at fine butchers, some specialty food stores, or by mail order from D'Artagnan (see Sources).

TUNA TARTARE ON RICE CRACKERS WITH WASABI MAYONNAISE

MAKES 30 PIECES

Three 8 by 8-inch spring roll wrappers (see Note)
2 cups vegetable oil
1 cup fine-quality mayonnaise
1 tablespoon fresh lemon juice
2½ tablespoons wasabi paste, plus more to taste (see Note)
1 package radish sprouts, optional
1 pound sushi-grade tuna, cut into ¼-inch dice (see Note)
Approximately ½ cup Ginger-Soy Dipping Sauce (see page 233)
¼ cup hijiki seaweed, optional (see Note)
1 ounce wasabi caviar or green, orange, or red flavored flying fish roe,
*   optional (see Note)*

1. Leaving the spring roll wrappers in a stack and using a very sharp knife, cut 2- by 2-inch squares. You will need only 30 squares, but make extra pieces to allow for breakage. Separate the squares into single pieces and set aside.

2. Heat the oil to 365°F on a candy thermometer in a small saucepan over medium-high heat. Working with a few at a time, drop the rice paper squares into the hot oil. Fry for about 15 seconds or until crisp and golden. Using a slotted spoon, remove the crisp crackers from the oil and drain on paper towel.

3. Combine the mayonnaise with the lemon juice and 1 tablespoon of the wasabi paste in a small bowl. Cover and refrigerate until ready to use.

4. If using the radish sprouts as a garnish, trim off all but 1 inch off the top. (Use the bottom for salads or sandwiches.) Set the tops aside.

5. When ready to serve, mix the tuna with just enough Ginger-Soy Dipping Sauce to moisten it. Stir in the remaining wasabi paste to taste until well blended.

6. Spoon 1 tablespoon of the tuna mixture on top of each cracker. Garnish the top with a dollop of the reserved wasabi mayonnaise and, if desired, the reserved radish sprouts and a few strands of hijiki or with a small dot of wasabi caviar or flying fish roe. Serve immediately.

NOTE: Spring roll wrappers, wasabi paste, hijiki seaweed, wasabi caviar, and flavored flying fish roe are available at Asian markets and specialty food stores. Spring roll wrappers are also often available in supermarkets.

For ease in cutting, wrap the tuna in plastic wrap and place in the freezer for about 15 minutes. This will firm the meat and allow the knife to easily cut through it.

Combine the tuna with the sauce just before using or the acid in the sauce will begin to "cook" the tuna and the color will become unappetizing.

If the Asian garnishes seem a bit extravagant, just use a small cilantro or parsley leaf tucked into the tuna tartare for a bit of color.

CURRIED CRAB AND ZUCCHINI TEMPURA

MAKES 30 PIECES

2 large zucchini
3 large sea scallops
2 tablespoons olive oil
6 ounces fresh crabmeat, picked clean of all shell and cartilage
⅓ cup minced carrot
⅓ cup minced leek, white and light-green part only
⅓ cup minced celery
¼ cup curry powder
½ teaspoon cayenne pepper, or to taste
Coarse salt to taste
1½ cups tempura flour (see Note)
1 large carrot, peeled, trimmed, and cut into matchsticks
1 stalk celery, well washed, trimmed, and cut into matchsticks
1 large egg
5 ice cubes
Approximately ½ cup cold seltzer water
2 cups vegetable oil

1. Line two or three baking sheets with clean kitchen towels or a triple layer of paper towel. Trim and discard both ends from the zucchini. Cut the zucchini, lengthwise, into paper-thin slices. (This is best done on a Japanese vegetable slicer, mandoline, or meat slicer; see Note.) You will need 30 slices of equal size. Place the zucchini slices on the prepared baking sheets so that most of the seeping moisture is absorbed. You might have to pat the tops dry with paper towel.

2. Place the scallops in the bowl of a food processor fitted with the metal blade. With the motor running, slowly add the olive oil and process until smooth.

THE TRIBECA GRILL COOKBOOK

3. Combine the crabmeat, carrot, leek, and celery in a mixing bowl. Scrape the scallop puree into the crab mixture and stir to combine. Add 1 tablespoon of the curry powder along with the cayenne and salt to taste and stir to blend well.

4. Place the remaining curry powder and tempura flour on separate small plates.

5. Working with 1 strip at a time, place about 1 teaspoon of the crab mixture at the top of a zucchini strip. Stick the carrot and celery matchsticks into the mousse so that they extend outward. Roll the zucchini around the crab to make a neat cylinder, with matchsticks exploding out of the ends. The moist zucchini should stick together. Roll each cylinder in curry powder to very lightly coat. Set aside until all cylinders are prepared.

6. Whisk the egg in a small bowl. Add the ice cubes and stir in 1 cup of the tempura flour until well combined. When all the ice cubes have melted, add enough seltzer water to make the consistency of pancake batter. (If not using immediately, cover and refrigerate, as the batter must be very cold.)

7. Heat the vegetable oil in an 8-inch sauté pan over medium-high heat until it reads 350°F on a candy thermometer.

8. Working with a few at a time, roll each cylinder in the remaining tempura flour to lightly coat. Dip them into the ice-cold tempura batter and fry for about 1 minute or until golden and crisp. Drain on paper towel. Serve hot.

NOTE: A Japanese vegetable slicer is a very useful and inexpensive (about $30) kitchen tool. Its extremely sharp blade allows you to cut vegetables into paper-thin strips for salads, frying, or garnishes. It does much the same work as the substantially more expensive mandoline. Available at kitchen supply stores and at some Asian markets and specialty food stores.

Tempura flour is available at Japanese markets and some specialty food stores.

This typically Asian fried tempura is best served freshly made and piping hot.

Wild Mushroom Risotto "Bombs"

Makes 30 cakes

1 large carrot, trimmed and peeled
1 cup plus 1 tablespoon olive oil
1 tablespoon minced garlic
1 cup cremini mushrooms, cleaned and finely chopped
1 cup oyster mushrooms, cleaned and finely chopped
1 cup small button mushrooms, cleaned and finely chopped
Approximately 4 cups Vegetable Stock (see page 230)
½ cup (1 stick) unsalted butter, at room temperature
½ cup finely diced onion
2 cups Arborio rice
½ cup freshly grated Parmesan cheese
Coarse salt and freshly ground white pepper to taste
3 large eggs
2 tablespoons milk
2 cups Italian-seasoned bread crumbs

1. Cut the carrot, lengthwise, into paper-thin slices on a Japanese vegetable slicer or mandoline (see page 19). Using a very sharp knife, cut 30 extremely thin 2-inch-long pieces. (These carrot strands will serve as the "fuses" for the risotto "bombs.") Place the strands in ice water to cover and set aside.

2. Heat 1 tablespoon of the olive oil in a large sauté pan over medium heat. Add the garlic and sauté for 1 minute. Stir in the mushrooms and cook, stirring frequently, for about 12 minutes or until the mushrooms are tender and lightly browned and all of the liquid has evaporated. Remove from the heat and set aside.

3. Place the Vegetable Stock in a medium saucepan over medium heat and bring to a simmer. Lower the heat to just keep the broth hot.

THE TRIBECA GRILL COOKBOOK

"**M**y usual traditional risotto cakes became 'bombs' for a wrap party in honor of the completion of Bob's Rocky and Bullwinkle movie. Since the movie incorporated explosives and technological wizardry, and I often try to create a theme with food that will reflect the event, I had to improvise many a turn on tradition for this one. I thought that we should have fun exploiting these much-loved cartoon characters with some funny food items. With this hors d'oeuvre, you have an example of something very classic being made into an amusing, talked-about hors d'oeuvre that expressed the theme of an event."

Wild Mushroom Risotto "Bombs" (left front and right rear),
Curried Crab and Zucchini Tempura (right front and left rear)

4. Heat 2 tablespoons of the butter in a medium heavy-bottomed saucepan over medium-low heat. Add the onion and cook, stirring frequently, for about 7 minutes or until the onion has sweat most of its liquid but has not taken on any color. Add the rice and sauté for about 4 minutes or until the rice is glistening with a nice coating of butter. Add 2 tablespoons of butter and 1 cup of the hot broth. Cook, stirring constantly with a wooden spoon, until the liquid has been absorbed by the rice. Continue adding broth, 1 cup at a time, stirring and cooking until the liquid has been absorbed and the rice is very creamy

and al dente. Stir in the Parmesan cheese and remaining butter along with the reserved mushrooms. Taste and adjust the seasoning with salt and white pepper. Remove from the heat and allow to cool.

5. Place the eggs in a small bowl and whisk in the milk.

6. Place the bread crumbs on a plate.

7. Using your hands, shape the cooled risotto into 30 small "bombs" about 1-inch-plus in diameter. (You may not use all of the risotto.) One at a time, dip the "bombs" into the egg mixture and then roll them in the bread crumbs. Set aside.

8. Heat the remaining olive oil to 360°F on a candy thermometer in a large sauté pan over medium heat. Add the risotto "bombs," a few at a time, and fry for about 1 minute per side or until crispy and golden brown. Drain well on paper towels. (You may want to place the "bombs" in a warm oven to keep them hot as you fry the remaining cakes.)

9. Remove the carrot strands from the ice water and pat dry.

10. Using a toothpick, make a tiny hole in the top of each "bomb" and insert a reserved carrot "fuse" into each one. Serve hot.

NOTE: If cremini and/or oyster mushrooms aren't available, substitute any other wild mushrooms, or, if no wild mushrooms are in season, use only button mushrooms. The risotto will not be quite as aromatic but it will still be delicious.

The risotto may be made a day in advance and formed into "bombs." Bread the "bombs" early on the day of use. Fry them a couple of hours in advance of use and reheat in a 350°F oven just before serving. The "bombs" may also be made well in advance of use and stored, well wrapped and frozen. Thaw and reheat as above on the day of use. (The risotto may also be formed into cakes about 2 inches in diameter and ½ inch thick.)

 THE TRIBECA GRILL COOKBOOK

LOBSTER AND MANGO TARTLETS

MAKES 30 TARTLETS

*1 package frozen phyllo dough, thawed according to
    manufacturer's directions*
½ cup (1 stick) unsalted butter, melted
1 pound cooked lobster meat, diced
1 large ripe mango, peeled and finely diced
1 small red bell pepper, cored, seeded, and finely diced
½ cup finely diced red onion
¼ cup minced fresh cilantro leaves
½ teaspoon minced jalapeño chile, or to taste
Juice of 3 limes
¼ cup olive oil
2 tablespoons white wine vinegar
Coarse salt to taste
¼ cup julienned scallion greens

1. Preheat the oven to 350°F.

2. Set out one large minimuffin tin or two small minimuffin tins (enough to make at least 30 phyllo cups).

3. Lay the phyllo dough out on a slightly damp kitchen towel and cover it with another barely damp towel. Keep the dough covered as you work to keep it from drying out. Carefully pull off one sheet of dough and lay it out on a clean surface. Using a pastry brush, lightly coat the dough with melted butter. Cover with another sheet of phyllo and brush it with melted butter. Continue making layers in this fashion until you have 8 buttered layers of phyllo.

4. Cut the dough into 2-inch squares and fit each square into an individual mini-muffin cup, pushing down on the sides to make a firm fit and to create a basket shape. Weight each basket down with a few pastry weights (or dried beans or peas) to help keep its shape as it bakes. Continue layering phyllo and cutting squares until you have 30 baskets. (You might want to make a few extra to allow for breakage.) Place in the preheated oven and bake for about 12 minutes or until crisp and golden. Remove from the heat and allow to cool. When cool, carefully remove the weights (or beans or peas). Leave the baskets in the muffin tins for ease in filling.

5. Combine the lobster, mango, red pepper, onion, cilantro, and jalapeño. Add the lime juice, oil, vinegar, and salt to taste. Toss to combine. Cover and refrigerate until ready to use.

6. When ready to serve, place 1 tablespoon of the lobster mixture into each phyllo basket. Garnish with some julienned scallion greens and serve immediately.

NOTE: The lobster can be replaced by cooked shrimp, crab, or any firm-fleshed fish or roast pork or chicken.

As long as the weather is dry, the phyllo baskets can be made early in the day and left in the muffin tins until ready to use.

The lobster mixture can also be made early in the day and stored, covered and refrigerated.

"In the 1940s, Francis Ford Coppola's father, Carmen, created the original music for the silent film *Napoleon*. In 1997, Francis asked the chefs from our group (Tribeca Grill, Nobu, Layla, Montrachet, and Rubicon) to join forces and create a menu for the release party celebrating his remake of the movie. The dinner, for seven hundred people, was held at Francis's home and winery, the former Inglenook estate in northern California. Movie seats were brought outdoors and, after dinner, the silent movie, scored by Francis's father, was shown. Instead of the usual movie house organ, the music was played by a twenty-piece orchestra, under a beautiful indigo-blue California sky. It truly was an evening to remember. What better hors d'oeuvre to start the celebration than a made-for-the-evening Tribeca Grill napoleon?"

GOAT CHEESE AND OVEN-DRIED TOMATO NAPOLEONS

MAKES 30 PIECES

*2 tablespoons minced fresh flat-leaf
    parsley leaves*
2 tablespoons minced fresh tarragon leaves
2 tablespoons minced fresh thyme leaves
*Two 8-ounce, 1½-inch round logs fresh
    goat cheese*
24 ripe plum tomatoes
1 clove garlic, minced
3 tablespoons olive oil
*Coarse salt and freshly ground pepper
    to taste*
*2 sheets frozen puff pastry, thawed
    according to manufacturer's directions*
1 large egg, well beaten

1. Preheat the oven to 350°F.

2. Combine the parsley, tarragon, and thyme, separately reserving 1 tablespoon. Spread the larger portion of herbs out on a clean surface and roll the goat cheese log in them until well covered. Cover tightly with plastic wrap and refrigerate until ready to use.

3. Line two cookie sheets with parchment paper. Set aside.

4. Slice the tomatoes, crosswise, into ¼-inch-thick slices. You will need 120 slices of equal size. Place the slices in a small bowl and toss together with the reserved tablespoon of herbs and the garlic. Drizzle in the olive oil and season

to taste with salt and pepper. Lay the tomato slices out on one of the prepared cookie sheets. Place in the preheated oven and roast for 20 minutes or until the tomatoes are slightly dry and wilted. Remove from the oven and set aside. Do not turn off the oven.

5. Place the puff pastry on a lightly floured surface and poke the pastry with the tines of a dinner fork to keep it from rising. Using a 2-inch round biscuit (or cookie) cutter, cut out 90 pastry rounds, placing the pastry rounds on the remaining prepared cookie sheet and covering them with another cookie sheet (of a size equal to the bottom sheet) on top of them to keep the dough from rising too much as you cut. When all of the rounds have been cut, using a pastry brush, lightly coat each pastry round with the beaten egg. Cover the egg-wash-coated pastry rounds with a sheet of parchment paper and, again, place another cookie sheet on top of them to keep the pastry from rising too much. Place the pastry into the preheated oven and bake for 30 minutes or until the pastry is crisp and golden brown. Remove the pastry from the oven and carefully place the rounds on wire racks to cool. (Do not turn off the oven but lower the heat to 300°F.) When cool, using a very sharp knife, cut each one in half, crosswise, to make 60 thin rounds.

6. Place 30 pastry rounds out on a clean surface.

7. Remove the goat cheese from the refrigerator and remove and discard the plastic wrap. Using a hot knife or a fine string, carefully cut the goat cheese into sixty ¼-inch-thick slices. Place a tomato slice on each of the thirty pastry circles and then a slice of goat cheese. Lay another slice of tomato on top of the goat cheese. Top with a pastry round and then with the tomato, goat cheese, and tomato layers. Top with the remaining pastry rounds. Place the napoleons on a cookie sheet in the preheated oven and bake for about 3 minutes or until the cheese is slightly melted. Serve immediately.

Somen Noodle and Vegetable "Sushi"

Makes 32 pieces

2 large red onions, peeled
2 cups rice wine vinegar (see Note)
1 cup water
½ cup sugar
5 juniper berries
4 medium spears of asparagus
1 carrot, peeled and julienned
1 leek, white and light-green part only, well washed and julienned
1 red bell pepper, cored, seeded, and julienned
8 ounces Japanese somen noodles (see Note)
2 tablespoons dark sesame oil (see Note)
4 sheets yaki nori (dried seaweed) (see Note)
1 cup Ginger-Soy Dipping Sauce (see page 233)
1⅓ tablespoons wasabi paste (see Note)

1. Slice the onions in half, lengthwise, and slice them on a Japanese vegetable slicer or mandoline (see page 19) into paper-thin slices. Set aside.

2. Combine the rice wine vinegar, water, sugar, and juniper berries in a medium nonreactive saucepan over medium heat. Bring to a boil and remove from the heat. Immediately add the onions and allow to cool to room temperature. Strain through a fine sieve, discarding the liquid. Place the onions in a nonreactive container. Cover and refrigerate until ready to use.

3. Trim the tough ends from the asparagus and, using a vegetable peeler, remove any tough skin. Each spear should be of equal size to the others. Set aside.

4. Fill a bowl with ice water and set it aside.

5. Bring 2 quarts of salted water to a boil in a large saucepan over high heat. Add the asparagus and boil for 1 minute. Using a slotted spoon, lift the asparagus spears from the boiling water and immediately immerse them in the ice water bath to stop the cooking.

6. Add the carrot, leek, and red pepper julienne to the boiling water and boil for 30 seconds. Using a slotted spoon, lift the julienned vegetables from the boiling water and immediately immerse them in the ice water bath to stop the cooking. Using a slotted spoon, lift all of the vegetables from the ice water bath and place them on paper towel to drain well.

7. Place the somen noodles in the boiling water and boil for 1 minute. Drain well and pat dry. Place the noodles in a large bowl. Add the sesame oil and toss to lightly coat the noodles.

8. Working with 1 piece at a time, lay the yaki nori, shiny side up, on a sushi mat (see Note) with the bamboo running horizontally. Using a pastry brush, lightly coat the nori with Ginger-Soy Dipping Sauce. Spread 1 cup of the seasoned somen noodles to evenly coat two thirds of the nori, allowing the noodles to extend ¼ inch beyond each side and leaving 1 inch of the top end of the nori uncovered. Arrange one quarter of the carrot, leek, and red pepper julienne and the pickled red onions horizontally across the noodles so that they also extend ¼ inch beyond each side of the nori. Spread ⅓ teaspoon of the wasabi paste on an asparagus spear and lay it on top of the vegetables.

9. Begin rolling up the "sushi" by lifting up the end of the mat closest to you and, pulling toward yourself, roll firmly

"One afternoon we got a telephone call from Linda McCartney asking if she and Paul could bring fifteen guests, that evening, for a strictly vegetarian dinner. I, of course, said 'No problem.' Normally, it wouldn't have been any trouble, but since it was two hours before she expected to arrive, I had to quickly organize an eight-course vegetarian menu from ingredients I had on hand. Instead of the usual Tribeca rare tuna with cold sesame noodles, I started the dinner with this dish—cold noodles, fresh vegetables, and pickled onions wrapped in nori and highlighted with a great dipping sauce. This is a perfect example of spontaneity in cooking—in this instance, we took a familiar dish and, with a few tweaks, turned it into a made-to-order appetizer. At the end of the evening, Linda asked for the recipe, which I gladly shared."

toward the top. Using a pastry brush, lightly coat the uncovered nori with Ginger-Soy Dipping Sauce. Use the 1 inch of uncovered nori to overlap and close the roll. Remove the sushi mat and continue making rolls until you have completed 4 nori-wrapped rolls. Refrigerate for 10 minutes.

10. Using a very sharp knife, neatly trim the ends of the roll. Cut each roll into 8 pieces and serve with Ginger-Soy Dipping Sauce on the side.

NOTE: Rice wine vinegar, somen noodles, dark sesame oil, yaki nori, wasabi paste, and sushi mats are available from Japanese markets, specialty food stores, and some supermarkets.

The sushi rolls may be made early in the day and stored, covered and refrigerated.

Mushroom Palmiers

Makes 30 pieces

2 tablespoons olive oil

3 small shallots, peeled and sliced

1 teaspoon minced garlic

1½ pounds assorted wild mushrooms (such as cremini, shiitake, oyster), cleaned and chopped

¼ cup dry white wine

¼ cup heavy cream

¼ cup minced fresh flat-leaf parsley leaves

Coarse salt and freshly ground pepper to taste

½ cup yellow cornmeal

1 tablespoon toasted mustard seeds

1 large egg

1 sheet frozen puff pastry, thawed

3 tablespoons truffle oil, optional (see Note)

"This is a vegetarian hors d'oeuvre created for the premiere party for *Truth or Dare*, Madonna's documentary film of her notorious tour. When it hit the theaters, she threw herself a party in the main dining room. Of course, once people realized that Madonna was there, everyone in the restaurant (including the staff) found an excuse to accidentally pass by her table hoping for a peek and an autograph. Madonna had made it clear that she would not be signing autographs during the evening, but a very sweet little Italian boy (who was dining in the restaurant with his family) had the courage to approach her. Madonna told him that if he could recite a poem, she would consider giving him her autograph. The little boy ran back to his parents and animatedly talked and gestured to them. He wrote something down and studied it intently. Then, he shyly returned to Madonna, stood in front of her and recited his words, in Italian. You could see her heart melt—an autograph and a hug were given and the little boy had his moment to remember."

1. To make mushroom duxelles, heat the olive oil in a large sauté pan over medium heat. Add the shallots and garlic and cook, stirring frequently, for about 3 minutes or until the shallots are tender. Stir in the mushrooms and lower the heat. Cook, stirring frequently, for about 10 minutes or until the mushrooms are well browned and quite dry. Add the wine and continue cooking, stirring frequently, for about 3 minutes or until the

moisture has evaporated. Add the cream and cook, stirring frequently, for about 3 minutes or until the mixture is almost dry. Stir in the parsley and season to taste with salt and pepper. Remove from the heat and set the duxelles aside to cool to room temperature.

2. When the mushroom mixture is cool, place it in the bowl of a food processor fitted with the metal blade and process until the mixture is finely minced. Set aside.

3. Combine the cornmeal and mustard seeds in a small bowl and set aside.

4. Place the egg in a small bowl and whisk in about 1 tablespoon of cold water. Set aside.

5. Lay the puff pastry out on a clean, flat surface. Working quickly and using a pastry brush, brush the top of the puff pastry with the egg wash. Sprinkle the cornmeal mixture over the pastry (*top photo*) and, using your palms, press it into the pastry. Flip the pastry over and spread the reserved mushroom mixture over it. Using a sharp knife, cut the pastry in half, lengthwise (*second photo*), making 2 rectangles of equal size.

6. Working with the long sides, roll each side about one quarter of the way toward the center (*third photo*); roll in again until both sides meet in the center. Repeat with the other rectangle. Place the folded pastry onto a cookie sheet and place in the freezer until very firm. (Do not omit the freezing or the palmiers will not cook properly.)

7. Preheat the oven to 375°F.

8. Line two cookie sheets with parchment paper. Set aside.

9. Cut the folded pastry, crosswise, into ¼-inch-thick slices. Place the pastry slices on the prepared cookie sheets without crowding (*bottom photo*). Place in the preheated oven and bake for 15 minutes or until crisp and golden brown. If desired, drizzle with truffle oil and serve warm.

NOTE: The mushroom duxelles may be made 2 days in advance of use. Cover and refrigerate until needed.

Once the pastry is firm, the palmiers may be cut into slices and frozen. Place them in resealable plastic bags, label, and freeze for up to 6 months. Bake directly from the freezer.

Truffle oil is available from Italian markets or specialty food stores.

"The very first party given at Tribeca Grill, held in celebration of Liza Minnelli's wedding anniversary, occurred before we were open. Because the kitchen was not yet finished, we hired two U-Hauls, which were placed end to end with propane-fired stoves lining the interior to use as satellite kitchens. This still left me without a place to prep the food, so I borrowed a friend's New Jersey catering kitchen and asked him to help me.

"On the day of the party, a Japanese chef friend arrived for a visit. Needing all the help I could find, I picked him up at the airport and put him right to work. It goes without saying we were running late and didn't leave the kitchen until 3:00 P.M. for the six o'clock dinner in New York. As we pulled up to the entrance to the Holland Tunnel, I reached for my wallet, which I quickly realized was back at the kitchen. I asked my caterer friend to spot me the $4 for the toll, only to discover that he didn't have any money either. That left my Japanese visitor, who only had yen. Nothing to do but beg for mercy. The toll taker wasn't having any of our story and made us turn around. We had no time to go back, so we tried another toll lane. No way. We tried the police guard. He was ready to arrest me as I tried to sell him a couple of my knives in exchange for toll money. I finally saw a rather unsavory-looking guy walking toward the far side of the tunnel entrance. I grabbed three of my knives (worth about $200) and asked if he was interested in buying them for $10: 'What else you got, man?' He ended up getting ten pounds of cookies, a selection of hors d'oeuvres and antipasti, and my knives. We got through the tunnel with $6 to spare. And we made it with enough time to pull the party off without a hitch. And Liza Minnelli never knew that I sold my knives just for her. So began party time at the Tribeca Grill."

SPINACH AND FETA IN PHYLLO

MAKES 30 PIECES

3 tablespoons olive oil
2 tablespoons minced garlic
2 pounds fresh spinach, leaves only, well washed and dried
½ pound feta cheese, crumbled
3 large eggs, beaten
1 cup toasted slivered almonds
Coarse salt and freshly ground pepper to taste
*1 package frozen phyllo dough, thawed according to manufacturer's
   directions*
2 cups (1 pound) unsalted butter, melted

1. Heat the olive oil in a large saucepan over medium heat. Add the garlic and
    sauté for 3 minutes or until just beginning to take on some color. Immediately
    add the spinach and cook, tossing frequently, for about 4 minutes or until the
    spinach is completely wilted. Transfer to a colander and, using a spatula, press
    out all of the liquid.

2. Place the drained spinach on a clean, dry surface and, using a sharp knife,
    coarsely chop. Place the spinach in a medium mixing bowl and add the cheese
    and eggs. Stir to blend well. Add the almonds and season to taste with salt and
    pepper. Set aside.

3. Preheat the oven to 375°F.

4. Line two cookie sheets with parchment paper. Set aside.

5. Lay the phyllo dough out on a slightly damp kitchen towel and cover it with
    another barely damp towel. Keep the dough covered as you work to keep it
    from drying out. Carefully pull off 1 sheet of dough and lay it out on a clean sur-
    face. Using a pastry brush, lightly coat the dough with melted butter. Cover

with another sheet of phyllo and brush it with melted butter. Continue making layers until you have 5 buttered sheets of phyllo. You will need to make 6 stacks.

6. Using a sharp knife, cut the buttered phyllo in half, crosswise; cut each half, lengthwise, into 2-inch strips. (You will get 4 to 5 strips from each stack of phyllo.)

7. Spoon 2 teaspoons of the spinach filling onto the center of the bottom end of each strip. Roll up the strip into a triangle shape, by folding the lower-right-hand corner of the strip over the filling to the opposite side. Continue to fold, flag-folding style, until you reach the top of the strip. Gently press the end of the phyllo to the underneath side. Place the finished triangles on the prepared baking sheets.

8. You will have to repeat Steps 5, 6, and 7 five times to make 30 triangles. Because phyllo tends to dry out, it is best to work with one group of strips at a time.

9. When all of the triangles are complete, lightly brush the tops with melted butter. Place in the preheated oven and bake for 8 minutes or until the phyllo is golden brown and the filling is hot and bubbly. Serve immediately.

NOTE: This is a rather traditional Greek-style filling for phyllo hors d'oeuvres. You could, however, fill the phyllo triangles with the mushroom duxelles used for the palmiers (see page 30), the Venison Empanada filling (see page 35), or any other slightly dry meat or vegetable filling. In fact, you can use almost any filling except one that is very juicy, as the moisture will make the phyllo soggy.

VENISON EMPANADAS WITH CHARRED TOMATO SALSA

MAKES 30 PIECES

3¾ cups sifted all-purpose flour
½ cup sugar
Pinch of coarse salt, plus more to taste
½ cup (1 stick) unsalted butter, at room temperature
1 cup plus 2 tablespoons water
2 tablespoons olive oil
1 medium red onion, peeled and finely diced
2 cloves garlic, peeled and minced
½ cup port wine
1 pound ground venison meat (see Note)
1 cup Beef Stock (see Note, page 230) or canned beef broth
1 cup diced, peeled, and seeded plum tomatoes
½ cup dried currants
¼ cup chopped fresh flat-leaf parsley
Freshly ground pepper to taste
1 large egg, beaten with 2 tablespoons cold water
Charred Tomato Salsa, optional (recipe follows)

1. Combine the flour, sugar, and salt in the bowl of a food processor fitted with the metal blade. Add the butter and, using quick on and off turns, process to incorporate. Slowly add the water and process until a smooth dough forms. Remove the dough from the processor bowl and form it into a flat disk. Wrap in plastic wrap and refrigerate for 8 hours.

2. To make the filling, heat the olive oil in a large sauté pan over medium heat. Add the onion and garlic and sauté for 4 minutes. Add the port wine and bring to a boil. Cook, stirring frequently, for about 5 minutes or until the wine has evaporated. Add the venison and sauté for 2 minutes or until the venison

begins to take on some color. Add the stock or broth, tomatoes, and currants and lower the heat. Cook, stirring frequently, for about 15 minutes or until the liquid has evaporated and the flavors are well blended. Stir in the parsley and season to taste with salt and pepper.

3. When ready to bake, preheat the oven to 350°F and line two cookie sheets with parchment paper.

4. Remove the chilled dough from the refrigerator. Unwrap and place on a lightly floured surface. Roll the dough out to a ⅛-inch thickness. Using a 2-inch round cookie or biscuit cutter, cut out 30 pastry circles.

5. Place 1 tablespoon of the venison filling in the center of each of the pastry circles. Using a pastry brush, lightly coat the edges of the pastry with egg wash. Fold one half of the dough over the filling and press the edges together with your fingers to make a half-moon shape. Using a dinner fork, crimp the edges of the dough together to make a decorative edging.

6. Lay the finished empanadas on the prepared cookie sheets. Using the pastry brush, lightly coat the top of each empanada with egg wash. Place in the preheated oven and bake for 15 minutes or until golden. Remove from the oven and serve hot with Charred Tomato Salsa, if desired.

"When the premiere party for *Like Water for Chocolate* was scheduled to take place at Tribeca Grill, the director sent me an advance copy of the film so I could get a sense of the food in the film. With dishes like quail with rose petals and aphrodisiac mole sauce, I didn't know if I could match the movie's culinary creativity! I wanted to create something fabulous, so I enlisted the help of my South American chefs, Luis Branez and Edgar Bran, to assist in putting a Latin spin on things. We re-created many of the foods from the film and improvised others in the style of the movie. These empanadas have since moved, like water for chocolate, from that event into our repertoire."

CHARRED TOMATO SALSA

MAKES ABOUT 2 CUPS

8 plum tomatoes, well washed and halved lengthwise
3 cloves garlic, peeled
2 red onions, peeled and quartered

*2 jalapeño chiles, well washed, stemmed, and halved
    lengthwise
¼ cup olive oil
Coarse salt and freshly ground pepper to taste
3 chipotle chiles in adobo (see Note)
½ cup fresh cilantro leaves*

1. Preheat the oven to 375°F.

2. Combine the tomatoes, garlic, onions, and chiles in a medium baking dish.
    Add the olive oil and salt and pepper to taste. Toss to coat well. Place in the
    preheated oven and roast for about 40 minutes or until the vegetables are
    nicely charred. Remove from the oven and allow to cool to room temperature.

3. Place the cooled vegetable mixture into the bowl of a food processor fitted
    with the metal blade. Add the chipotles in adobo and cilantro and process
    until smooth. Taste and adjust seasoning with salt and pepper.

4. When ready to serve, place the sauce in a small nonreactive saucepan over
    medium heat and cook, stirring frequently, for about 3 minutes or just until
    warm. Serve warm.

NOTE: The empanada dough may be frozen. Cover tightly in plastic wrap, place in
a resealable plastic bag, label, and freeze for up to 6 months. Unwrap and thaw to
room temperature when ready to use.

Venison is available at fine butcher shops, some specialty food stores, or by
mail order from D'Artagnan (see Sources). In this recipe, any meat or poultry could
be used as a substitute if you have difficulty finding venison.

Chipotle chiles in adobo are a canned Mexican product available at Latin
American markets, specialty food stores, and some supermarkets.

The Charred Tomato Salsa may be made up to 1 week in advance of use.
Store, tightly covered and refrigerated. Reheat as above.

Appetizers
and Salads

APPETIZERS

BILL'S GREAT WALL OF TUNA

SMOKED SALMON WITH CREPES VONNASIENNES

CRAB CAKES WITH PICKLED MELON AND SPICY RÉMOULADE

SHRIMP AND VEGETABLE SPRING ROLLS WITH
SWEET AND SOUR SAUCE

SAUTÉ OF FOIE GRAS WITH PARSNIPS AND SOUR CHERRIES

PROSCIUTTO-WRAPPED FIGS WITH TRUFFLE CHEESE

SALADS

ARUGULA SALAD WITH BOCCONCINI

ENDIVE AND WATERCRESS SALAD

LEMON THYME CHICKEN SALAD WITH BEEFSTEAK TOMATOES

LAVENDER-SKEWERED SCALLOPS WITH WHITE BEAN
AND SHRIMP SALAD

CRISP FRIED OYSTERS WITH ASIAN VEGETABLE SLAW
AND GARLIC-ANCHOVY AÏOLI

BILL'S GREAT WALL OF TUNA

SERVES 6

THIS IS BILL MURRAY'S FAVORITE DISH—hence the name. It has been on the Tribeca Grill menu since our opening day. The recipe evolved from my cooking experiences in Japan, where I spent my days off visiting temples in nearby Kyoto and eating wonderfully refreshing cold noodles in a clear, delicate broth. It is the perfect dish that combines all of the flavors of Japan.

¼ cup hijiki seaweed (see Note)
1 package Japanese somen noodles (see Note)
1 cup plus 2 tablespoons Ginger-Soy Dipping Sauce (see page 233)
¼ cup Sesame Vinaigrette (see page 232)
Coarse salt and freshly ground pepper to taste
1 sheet yaki nori (see Note)
1 pound sashimi-grade tuna, cut into a 1½ by 1 by 10-inch
    rectangular log (see Note)
1 carrot, trimmed, peeled, and julienned
1 large head frisée, well washed, trimmed, and pulled apart
1 cup Preserved Mushrooms (see page 236)
1 cup Pickled Onions (see page 237)
1 red bell pepper, cored, seeded, and cut into fine dice
1 cup julienned red radish
2 tablespoons black sesame seeds (see Note)
1 cup radish sprouts

> **WINE:** The sesame and soy flavors are nicely balanced by the sweet, spicy qualities of an Alsatian Gewürztraminer such as one of the straightforward dry and crisp wines from P. Blanck or Zind-Humbrecht.

1. Place the hijiki in a bowl with warm water to cover by 2 inches. Allow to soak for 30 minutes; drain well. Cover and set aside.

2. Drop the noodles in a large pot of boiling salted water and return to a boil. Boil for 1 minute or until just tender, stirring constantly to keep the noodles from sticking. Drain well. Immediately cover with cold water and again drain well. Place the noodles in a large bowl and season with 2 tablespoons of the

Ginger-Soy Dipping Sauce and 1 teaspoon of the Sesame Vinaigrette. Taste and adjust the seasoning with salt and pepper. Set aside.

3. Lay the nori out on a clean, flat surface and, using a pastry brush, lightly coat with some of the remaining Ginger-Soy Dipping Sauce. Season the tuna with salt and pepper to taste and lay it across the bottom of the seasoned nori. Gently roll up to enclose the tuna with the nori.

4. Heat a nonstick sauté pan over high heat until very hot but not smoking. Add the tuna roll and sear for about 1 to 2 minutes or just until the tuna changes slightly in color from reddish-purple to light brown. Immediately remove from the heat and place in the refrigerator to cool.

5. When ready to serve, combine the carrot and frisée in a large bowl. Add the remaining vinaigrette. Toss together and season to taste with salt and pepper.

6. Place the frisée mixture in the center of each of six plates. Top the salad with an equal portion of the Preserved Mushrooms and Pickled Onions, diced bell pepper, radish julienne, and reserved soaked hijiki. Divide the reserved seasoned noodles into 6 equal portions. Working with 1 portion at a time, lay a portion in the palm of your hand and, using a fork, twirl the noodles in circles to make a long roll. Place the noodle roll along the edge of the salad. Sprinkle black sesame seeds around the edge of each plate.

7. Using a very sharp knife, cut the tuna roll into very thin slices. Place equal portions of the tuna (you should have at least 5 slices per plate) on the salad on each plate. Drizzle some of the reserved Ginger-Soy Dipping Sauce over the tuna. Garnish the plates with radish sprouts and serve.

NOTE: Hijiki seaweed, somen noodles, yaki nori, and black sesame seeds are available from Japanese markets and some specialty food stores.

Sashimi-grade tuna is available from fine fishmongers or by mail order from Browne Trading (see Sources).

There is nothing like the Great Wall of Tuna."—Bill Murray

Smoked Salmon with Crepes Vonnasiennes

SERVES 6

CREPES VONNASIENNES ARE A LEGACY from my time at Restaurant Georges Blanc in Vonnas, France, where I trained in the mid-eighties. The restaurant has been a family-owned dining spot for over one hundred years. The crepes were always served as a side dish there, but because they are so light and delicate, I find them to be a marvelous accent to smoked fish, carpaccios, and chicken. My version is adapted slightly for American ingredients.

2 Idaho potatoes, peeled and diced
¼ cup warm heavy cream
2 tablespoons unsalted butter, melted
Coarse salt and freshly ground black pepper to taste
2 large eggs, beaten
2 teaspoons potato starch
½ cup crème fraîche (see Note, page 77)
18 thin slices smoked salmon
1 cup Lemon-Caper Vinaigrette (see page 231)
2 cups mixed baby salad greens, well washed and dried
1 ounce osetra caviar
2 tablespoons chopped fresh chives

WINE: An Oregon Pinot Gris like the reserve bottling from King Estate has the creaminess and body to pair with the richness of the crepe and the proper acidity to cut through the oiliness of the smoked salmon.

1. Place the potatoes in a medium saucepan with cold, salted water to cover. Place over high heat and bring to a boil. Lower the heat and simmer for about 15 minutes or until the potatoes are very tender but not mushy. Drain well. Either pass the potatoes through a food mill or mash with a manual potato masher. Beat in the cream and butter and season to taste with salt and pepper.

2. Combine the eggs with the potato starch in a small bowl. When well blended, beat the egg mixture into the potatoes, mixing until very smooth. If the mixture is thicker than pancake batter, adjust it with an additional egg. Set aside.

3. Using an electric mixer, beat the crème fraîche until soft peaks form. Set aside.

4. Place 3 slices of salmon, slightly overlapping, on each of six luncheon plates. Using a pastry brush, lightly coat the salmon with some of the Lemon-Caper Vinaigrette.

5. Toss the greens with just enough of the vinaigrette to lightly coat them. (You may not use all of the vinaigrette.) Place a small mound of dressed greens at the top (twelve o'clock) of each plate.

6. Heat a nonstick griddle over medium heat. Spray lightly with nonstick vegetable spray. Drop the potato batter by the tablespoonful to make 18 cakes, each the size of a half-dollar. When bubbles appear on the surface of the batter, using a spatula, flip the crepes and cook for about 1 minute or until the remaining side is brown (see Note).

7. Place 3 warm crepes on each plate, leaning them onto the greens. Make a quenelle (see Note) of whipped crème fraîche and place it at the five o'clock position on the plate. Garnish the crème fraîche with a touch of caviar. Sprinkle chopped chives around the edge of the plate and serve.

NOTE: The Crepes Vonnasiennes (potato crepes) may be made in advance and stored, separated by wax paper, tightly sealed. Reheat in a preheated 350°F oven.

"Quenelle," a classic French oval-shaped dumpling, is the term also used to describe the oval shape itself. At Tribeca Grill, we gather the ingredient to be formed into a "quenelle" into two teaspoons and then form the shape by turning the spoons back and forth against the ingredient to form a smooth, oval shape that makes a very elegant statement on the plate. To practice forming a quenelle, place two teaspoons in hot water and then gather up a small amount of ice cream and turn the spoons against it until you get a perfect oval shape.

If caviar seems a bit extravagant, garnish the top with some chopped chives or scallions, tiny chive points or blossoms, or cracked black pepper.

CRAB CAKES WITH PICKLED MELON AND SPICY RÉMOULADE

SERVES 6

BY NOW, I GUESS ALMOST EVERY AMERICAN CHEF has his or her own version of the classic Maryland crab cake. This is mine, which I think has great balance of flavor with the accent of the sweet-tart Pickled Melon, the slight heat of the rémoulade, and the crunch of the panko bread crumbs.

1 pound jumbo lump crabmeat, picked clean of all
*   shell and cartilage*
1 large egg, beaten
½ cup fine-quality mayonnaise
½ cup finely diced red onion
½ cup finely diced red bell pepper
½ cup chopped fresh flat-leaf parsley leaves
1 tablespoon Dijon mustard
Juice of 2 lemons
1 teaspoon cayenne pepper
1 teaspoon paprika
Tabasco sauce to taste
Coarse salt to taste
One 6-ounce bag Japanese panko
*   bread crumbs (see Note)*
¼ cup vegetable oil
2 tablespoons unsalted butter
24 slices Pickled Melon (recipe follows)
Spicy Rémoulade (see page 234)
2 tablespoons chopped fresh chives

> **WINE:** An elegant, flavorful California Chardonnay from a producer such as Dehlinger or Neyers has the richness to pair with the sweet crab.

1. Crumble the crab into a mixing bowl. Add the egg and mayonnaise along with the onion, bell pepper, parsley, and mustard. Pour the lemon juice over the top and add the cayenne, paprika, and Tabasco and salt to taste. Using a fork, toss to barely combine. Add just enough bread crumbs to make a firm, moist mixture. Try not to overmix or the finished crab cakes will be mushy. Form the crab mixture into 12 small patties of equal size. Roll the crab cakes in the remaining bread crumbs and set aside.

2. Preheat the oven to 400°F.

3. Heat the vegetable oil in a nonstick, ovenproof sauté pan over medium-high heat. Add the crab cakes and fry for 2 minutes or until golden. Add the butter to the pan and turn the crab cakes over. Place in the preheated oven and bake for about 8 minutes or until the cakes are golden brown and cooked through. Remove from the oven and place on paper towel to drain.

4. Place 4 slices of Pickled Melon on each of six plates. Place 2 crab cakes on the top of the melon. Place dots of the Spicy Rémoulade around the edge of the plates and on the top of each crab cake (see Note). Sprinkle chives over each plate and serve.

PICKLED MELON

1 large, firm honeydew melon, peeled, seeded,
    and cut into 6 wedges of equal size
1 cup rice wine vinegar (see Note)
1 cup cold water
¼ cup mirin (Japanese rice wine) (see Note)
¼ cup sake (see Note)
1½ tablespoons sriracha (smooth Thai chili paste) (see Note)
2 teaspoons honey

1. Place the melon in a single layer in a shallow baking dish.

2. Combine the vinegar, water, mirin, sake, sriracha, and honey in a large, shallow (rondeau-shaped), nonreactive saucepan over medium heat. Bring to a

boil. Remove from the heat and pour the hot liquid over the reserved melon. Cover and allow to marinate until cool.

3. When cool, remove the melon from the liquid. Cut each wedge into ⅛-inch-thick slices and serve. Alternately, place the ⅛-inch slices in a nonreactive container, cover with the cooled liquid, and store, tightly covered and refrigerated, for up to 1 week.

NOTE: Sriracha, mirin, and rice wine vinegar are available from Japanese markets and some specialty food stores.

Panko bread crumbs are slightly sweetened Japanese-style bread crumbs that give a very crisp coating. I frequently use them with seafood as, to me, they give a sense of freshness and vibrancy to the finished dish. They are available from Japanese markets and some specialty food stores.

You might wish to place the rémoulade in a plastic squeeze bottle with a fine tip, such as those used for ketchup or mustard. Since it is a slightly textured sauce, you might have to cut the tip off to broaden the opening somewhat. Using the plastic squeeze bottle makes garnishing a plate with any sauce much, much easier, as you have greater control over the flow.

Sake is available from fine-quality liquor stores.

Shrimp and Vegetable Spring Rolls with Sweet and Sour Sauce

SERVES 6

THESE ALMOST CLASSIC CHINESE-STYLE spring rolls have been on and off the Tribeca Grill menu with great frequency. They evolved out of my time in Southeast Asia, but I sometimes think that they have their roots in all the take-out Chinese food I've eaten in New York! All in all, they are a straightforward spring roll with lots of Asian flavor and a great Sweet and Sour Sauce.

¼ cup sesame oil
1 teaspoon minced garlic
1 large carrot, peeled, trimmed, and grated
1 medium zucchini, trimmed and grated
1 medium yellow summer squash, trimmed and grated
3 cups shredded cabbage
2 teaspoons rice wine vinegar (see Note)
2 teaspoons nam pla (Thai fish sauce) (see Note)
1 teaspoon sriracha (smooth Thai chili paste) (see Note)
Coarse salt and freshly ground pepper to taste
12 spring roll wrappers (see Note)
12 poached jumbo shrimp, peeled and deveined
1 large egg, beaten
Approximately 6 cups vegetable oil
1 cup Sweet and Sour Sauce (see page 233)

WINE: The sugary flavor of the sauce requires a wine that combines both sweetness and acidity, such as a Tokay Pinot Gris from Ernest Brun. Its ripeness and crisp finish will keep the pairing at a nice balance.

1. Heat the sesame oil in a wok or large sauté pan over medium-high heat. Add the garlic and cook for 30 seconds. Stir in the grated vegetables and shredded cabbage and immediately add the vinegar, nam pla, and sriracha. Season to taste with salt and pepper and stir-fry for about 2 minutes or just until the vegetables are crisp-tender. (If necessary, stir-fry in batches to keep the vegetables

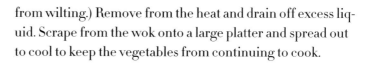

from wilting.) Remove from the heat and drain off excess liquid. Scrape from the wok onto a large platter and spread out to cool to keep the vegetables from continuing to cook.

2. Working with a few wrappers at a time, lay the wrappers out in a diamond shape. Place a heaping tablespoon of the cooled stir-fried vegetables in the center of the diamond, spreading them out into a line across the middle of the diamond shape. Place 1 shrimp on top of the vegetables on each wrapper and fold the bottom tip of the diamond up and over the shrimp to cover it. Fold in the two opposite side corners to encase the shrimp and vegetables (*top photo*). Using a pastry brush,

"Don swears that he is innocent—that he wasn't the person who set fire to the cashmere and mink scarf I left in the Tribeca Grill coat room—but the facts are pretty straightforward. One: Somebody set fire to my scarf. Two: The only person who had any reason to set fire to any of my personal belongings was Don.

"Here is what happened. Drew had invited me to Tribeca Grill to participate in a panel on restaurant reviewing, and I arrived with nothing prepared. The hostess—the one who took my scarf, as a matter of fact—asked me if I wanted anything to eat while I was waiting for the panel to begin. I ordered a Shrimp and Vegetable Spring Roll. You know how it is with shrimp and vegetable spring rolls—you order them in a Chinese restaurant and they never have any shrimp in them. Maybe if you dissect one, take it apart with tweezers and examine it with an electron microscope, you might find a tiny orange speck, something with the cell structure of plankton, but you never come across anything that a reasonable person would call shrimp. Don's spring roll was nothing but shrimp, oversized chunks of sweet rock shrimp, the most delicious shrimp spring roll I'd ever eaten. I realized immediately that it was a worthy topic of discussion.

"When I got upstairs, somebody in the audience asked me to explain how restaurant critics went about their business, and this is what I told him. I said that I'd just eaten the Shrimp and Vegetable Spring Roll at Tribeca Grill, and while it was quite tasty, my duty would be to write disapprovingly of it were I reviewing the restaurant, because it was devoid of vegetables. It was nothing but shrimp, a clear example of the kind of deceptive menu writing that every honest critic has a duty to stamp out.

"After the panel was over, I walked downstairs to get my coat, and the hostess told me that there had been an accident: My cashmere and mink scarf had a huge burn hole in it. To this day, I'm sure it was Don."

Alan Richman

lightly coat the remaining uncovered edges of the spring roll wrapper with the beaten egg. Tightly roll the wrapper into the top corner to make a nice, neat roll (*center photo*). Continue making spring rolls until you have 12 (*bottom photo*).

3. Heat the oil to 350°F in a deep-fat fryer over high heat. Add the spring rolls, a few at a time, and fry for about 3 minutes or until golden brown. Using a slotted spoon, lift the spring rolls from the oil and drain on paper towel. Continue frying until all 12 are cooked.

4. Cut the spring rolls in half, crosswise on the bias, and serve, 2 per person, with Sweet and Sour Sauce for dipping.

NOTE: Sesame oil, nam pla, sriracha, rice wine vinegar, and spring roll wrappers are available from Asian markets and some specialty food stores.

Prosciutto-Wrapped Figs with Truffle Cheese

SERVES 6

THIS IS A CLASSIC PIEDMONTESE COMBINATION of cheese and fruit made new by the addition of prosciutto. If you can get it, the Boscovivo adds a rich creaminess to the savory prosciutto and the sweet, ripe figs. But if it is not available, feel free to substitute other types of creamy cheeses, perhaps with a dash of truffle oil. Served individually, these figs make a great hors d'oeuvre.

13 Black Mission or other fresh figs
20 fresh mint leaves
1 tablespoon water
¼ cup plus 2 tablespoons olive oil
2 tablespoons white balsamic vinegar
6 ounces truffle cheese, such as Boscovivo
6 ounces prosciutto, very thinly sliced
¼ pound mâche, well washed and dried
Juice of 1 lemon
Coarse salt and freshly ground pepper to taste
2 tablespoons chopped fresh chives

WINE: The sweetness of the figs and the earthiness of the truffle cheese and prosciutto call for a wine that has concentrated fruitiness with an earthy finish, such as a hearty red from Spain's Ribero del Duero like Condado de Haza.

1. Cut 9 of the figs in half lengthwise. Set aside. Chop the remaining 4 figs and place them in a blender along with 2 of the mint leaves and the water. With the motor running, add ¼ cup of the olive oil and the vinegar. Process until smooth. Set aside.

2. Place the halved figs, cut side up, on a flat surface. Cut the cheese into 18 slices small enough to fit on top of each fig half. Place a slice of cheese on each fig and top with a mint leaf. Working with 1 fig half at a time, tightly wrap the prosciutto around it, trimming off any excess meat. Continue wrapping until all figs have been covered with prosciutto.

3. Heat a large, nonstick sauté pan over medium heat. Add the wrapped figs and sear for about 30 seconds or until the prosciutto is slightly crispy. Remove from the heat and set aside.

4. Toss the mâche with the lemon juice and remaining olive oil. Season to taste with salt and pepper. Place a mound of the salad in the center of each of six plates. Place 3 fig halves around the salad on each plate and drizzle some of the reserved fig sauce over all. Sprinkle chives over each plate and serve.

"I've always thought that the mark of a good, vibrant restaurant is when unexpected things happen. We would never expect, for instance, that 'New Yawkers' could have just as much 'Aloha' as Hawaiian Islanders. But Don and Drew have always opened their doors to myself and our chefs at Roy's. My fondest memories are of borrowing the Tribeca kitchen to prep for a dinner at the James Beard House, and having Don, personally, drive the food and supplies back and forth through the heavy traffic. Pintabona, the cabdriver, is a sight to behold! Then, there is the memory of Drew serenading me with his accordion while I was prepping.

"Since then, we've had Don and Drew over several times to the Islands to cook for our restaurants—always a larger-than-life experience. If only we could get them to stop wearing black socks with their tropical-weather clothes!"

Chef Roy Yamaguchi

The Tribeca Grill is on the corner of Greenwich and Franklin streets.

THE TRIBECA GRILL COOKBOOK

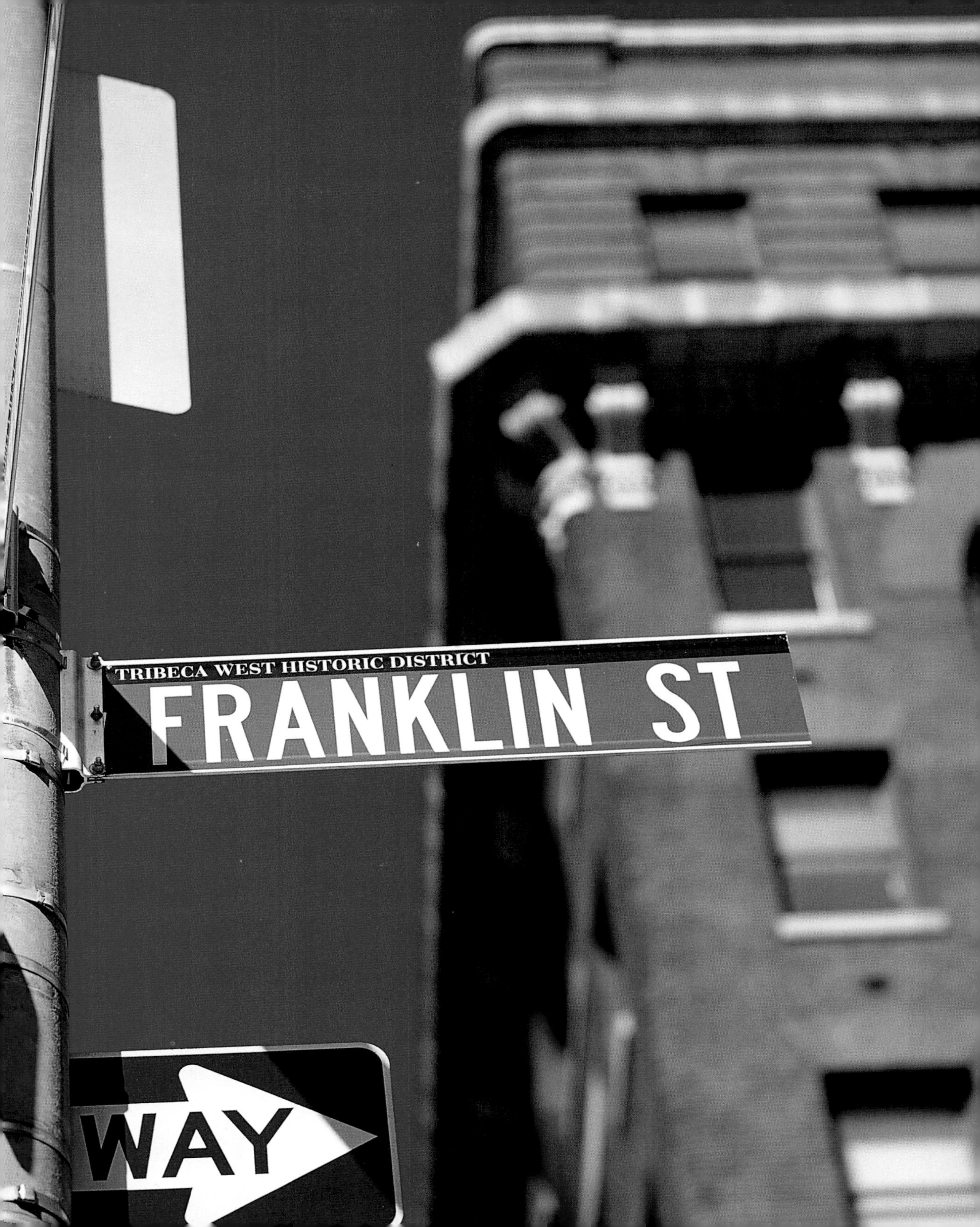
TRIBECA WEST HISTORIC DISTRICT
FRANKLIN ST
WAY

Arugula Salad with Bocconcini

SERVES 6

THIS IS A TRIBECA GRILL SIGNATURE DISH. It has been on the menu since day one. It is really a very simple salad made from a number of components with a spectacular presentation. However, since almost every component can be made well in advance of use—in fact most of the components are staples in the Tribeca pantry—it is no more difficult to put together than a plain old tossed salad. Just note that you will need a 3-inch plastic ring mold to create the Tribeca presentation.

1 ½ pounds bocconcini (see Note)
1 cup Garlic Oil (see page 235)
1 eggplant
¼ cup olive oil
Coarse salt and freshly ground pepper to taste
1 pound arugula, well washed and dried
1 cup Balsamic Vinaigrette (see page 232)
1 cup sliced Roasted Red Peppers (see page 238)
½ cup Oven-Dried Tomatoes (see page 238)
½ cup Tomato Fondue (see page 236)
½ cup Basil Oil (see page 236)
½ cup Tomato Oil (see page 236)
Cracked black pepper to taste

WINE: For a complex salad such as this, a high-acid, crisp Austrian wine like Grüner Veltliner from a fine producer such as Rudi Pichler or Hirsch would match many of the component flavors without overpowering the balance of the dish.

1. Drain the bocconcini and pat them dry. Place them in a shallow container and cover them with the Garlic Oil. Cover and refrigerate. Allow to marinate for at least 8 hours or up to 2 days.

2. Preheat the grill or a stovetop cast iron grill pan.

3. Trim the ends from the eggplant and slice it, lengthwise, into ¼-inch-thick

slices. Using a pastry brush, lightly coat the eggplant with the olive oil. Season to taste with salt and pepper. Place on the grill and cook, turning frequently, for about 5 minutes or until the eggplant is very tender but not falling apart. Remove from the grill and set aside to cool.

4. Place a 3-inch ring mold in the center of a salad plate. Using about 3 slices of eggplant, line the mold to form a solid base for the salad. Unless you have six 3-inch ring molds, you will have to do this six times.

5. Place the arugula in a mixing bowl and toss it with the Balsamic Vinaigrette. Taste and if necessary adjust the seasoning with salt and pepper. Divide the salad into 6 equal portions and stuff 1 portion into the eggplant-lined ring mold. Garnish the salad with a few slices of Roasted Red Pepper and Oven-Dried Tomatoes as well as 3 bocconcini. Carefully lift off the ring mold so that the salad keeps its shape. Continue making salads until you have 6.

6. Place 3 small quenelles (see Note on page 45) of Tomato Fondue at three equidistant points around the salad. Drizzle the Basil Oil and Tomato Oil around the edge of the plate. Shake a little cracked black pepper over the top and serve.

NOTE: Bocconcini, or small balls of freshly made mozzarella cheese, are available in Italian markets, cheese shops, specialty food stores, and some supermarkets.

OVERLEAF (FROM LEFT): Endive and Watercress Salad, Lavender-Skewered Scallops with White Bean and Shrimp Salad, Arugula Salad with Bocconcini, Lemon Thyme Chicken Salad with Beef-steak Tomatoes

"For the opening of Bob De Niro's film *A Bronx Tale*, we had a huge tent erected over the street to simulate an Italian street fair. There were eleven hundred invited guests with police guards and heavy security. The loading dock that fronts the restaurant was to serve rather like a balcony for the fair, but we didn't expect any of the guests to come into the restaurant itself, which was stripped bare for the event. Unfortunately, Bob headed for his usual table and everyone tried to follow him, which of course created chaos. Hollywood power agent Mike Ovitz, who could get nowhere near the place, was quoted as saying, 'There's nowhere to sit. There's nothing to drink. I can't get any food. No wonder it's such a success.' "

ENDIVE AND WATERCRESS SALAD

SERVES 6

THIS IS THE TRIBECA GRILL VERSION of a fairly standard French salad-green combination made interesting by the addition of the Glazed Walnuts and Americanized by the use of the marvelous Maytag Blue Cheese.

1 recipe Spiced Walnuts (see page 239)
½ pound watercress, tough stems removed, well washed and dried
¼ pound Maytag (or other fine-quality) Blue Cheese, crumbled
1 recipe Walnut Vinaigrette (see page 232)
2 Belgian endive
10 chives, sliced crosswise into thin circles
6 slices raisin-walnut bread, toasted and cut into triangles, optional

WINE: Ridge Lytton Springs Zinfandel has the concentration of fruit necessary to stand up to the pungent flavors of this salad. And with Zinfandel being a strictly American varietal, it is the logical match for the wonderful domestic Maytag Blue Cheese.

1. Divide the walnuts in half. Chop one half and separately reserve the chopped nuts from the halves. Set aside.

2. In a mixing bowl, combine the watercress, blue cheese, and reserved chopped nuts. Add just enough of the Walnut Vinaigrette to moisten the salad. Toss to coat well.

3. Cut the bottoms from the endive and then cut, lengthwise, into fine strips (see Note). Place in a mixing bowl and toss with half of the chives and enough vinaigrette to moisten. Make a ring of endive in the center of each of six plates. Place a handful of the watercress salad on top of the endive. Drizzle any remaining vinaigrette around the edge of the plates. Place 3 or 4 walnut halves on each plate and sprinkle the remaining chives over the top. Serve immediately with 2 triangles of raisin-walnut toast on each plate, if desired.

LEMON THYME CHICKEN SALAD WITH BEEFSTEAK TOMATOES

SERVES 6

JANE ROSENTHAL, ROBERT DE NIRO'S PARTNER in Tribeca Productions, kept requesting a healthy chicken salad for her take-out lunches. We finally prepared this prototype for one of her catered lunches and it was such a hit that we moved it onto our regular summer lunch menu. The unfortunate thing is that it can only be prepared during the height of summer, as perfection is met only when tomatoes are at their prime.

6 chicken breast halves poached in Court Bouillon (see page 231)
2 heads butterhead lettuce (such as Bibb or Boston), pulled apart, trimmed, well washed, and dried
½ pound fresh haricots verts (or tiny green beans), trimmed and blanched
12 cooked new potatoes, sliced ¼ inch thick crosswise
1 tablespoon fresh lemon thyme leaves
1 tablespoon chopped fresh chervil leaves
1 tablespoon chopped fresh chives
1 tablespoon chopped fresh flat-leaf parsley leaves
1 recipe Citrus Vinaigrette (see page 232)
Coarse salt and freshly ground pepper to taste
2 large red beefsteak tomatoes, cored and thinly sliced crosswise
2 large yellow beefsteak tomatoes, cored and thinly sliced crosswise (see Note)

WINE: The high acidity of vinaigrettes makes pairing wine with salad somewhat difficult. We most often choose a crisp, high-acid wine so that the acids cancel each other and the wine will taste softer. A light-bodied, crisp, citrus-scented Riesling from Australia's Leeuwin Estate or Bonny Doon Pacific Rim Riesling would match up nicely to this salad.

1. Using a very sharp knife, cut each breast half, on the bias, into very thin slices. Keep each breast half together. Set aside.

2. Combine the lettuce, haricots verts, potatoes, lemon thyme, chervil, chives, and parsley in a large mixing bowl. Add enough of the Citrus Vinaigrette to just moisten the salad. Taste and, if necessary, adjust the seasoning with salt and pepper.

3. Alternately place 3 slices of the red and 3 slices of the yellow tomatoes around one side of each of six plates. Season to taste with salt and pepper and drizzle a little vinaigrette over the tomatoes. Place a large handful of the salad in the center of each plate. Fan out 1 breast half over the salad on each plate. Drizzle some vinaigrette over the top and grind some black pepper over the plate. Serve immediately.

NOTE: If you can't find yellow beefsteak tomatoes, replace them with red. This will slightly alter the look of the salad but not the taste.

If you don't want to serve on individual plates, the salad makes a beautiful buffet platter with a ring of alternating red and yellow tomatoes around the edge of the dish, with the salad in the center.

Tribeca semolina dinner roll

LAVENDER-SKEWERED SCALLOPS WITH WHITE BEAN AND SHRIMP SALAD

SERVES 6

I LOVE THE SCENT OF PROVENCE that the lavender imparts to the salad and the subtly flavored scallops. However, if you can't find the lavender twigs, substitute the more available rosemary branches or even plain old bamboo skewers. The end result won't quite sing of the South of France, but the scent of lavender from the salad will add just enough of a French note to take you on an imaginary trip.

¼ cup olive oil
4 cloves garlic, peeled and chopped
2 shallots, peeled and chopped
½ pound shrimp, peeled, deveined, and cut into
  small pieces
Coarse salt and freshly ground pepper to taste
One 20-ounce can cannellini beans, well drained
1 stalk celery, trimmed, peeled, and finely diced
1 red bell pepper, cored, seeded, and finely diced
½ teaspoon dried lavender (see Note)
1¼ cups extra-virgin olive oil
¼ cup red wine vinegar
Juice of 2 lemons
12 large scallops
12 lavender twigs (see Note)
2 tablespoons chopped fresh flat-leaf parsley leaves

WINE: An oaky, well-balanced Chardonnay is required to marry with the richness of the seafood and, because of the earthiness of the white bean salad, the wine must also possess a clean, crisp finish. A white Burgundy such as Chassagne-Montrachet Les Masures from Jean-Noel Gagnard would do the trick.

1. Heat 2 tablespoons of the olive oil in a large sauté pan over medium heat. Add half of the garlic and half of the shallots and sauté for about 3 minutes or until slightly soft. Add the shrimp and sauté for an additional 3 minutes or until the shrimp is pink and cooked through. Season to taste with salt and pepper.

2. Combine the beans, celery, and bell pepper in a mixing bowl. Stir in the dried lavender and the remaining garlic and shallots. Add the cooked shrimp along with 1 cup of the extra-virgin olive oil, the vinegar, and lemon juice. Toss to combine. Taste and adjust the seasoning with salt and pepper. Transfer the salad to a large serving platter and set aside.

3. Cut each scallop in half, crosswise, to make 2 rounds of equal size. Thread 2 scallop circles onto each lavender twig. Heat the remaining 2 tablespoons olive oil in a large sauté pan over medium-high heat. Carefully lay the scallop skewers into the hot oil and cook, turning frequently, for about 2 minutes or until the scallops are lightly browned on all sides. Place scallop skewers on top of the salad. Drizzle the remaining ¼ cup extra-virgin olive oil around the edge of the platter. Sprinkle the chopped parsley over the top and serve.

NOTE: Dried lavender and lavender twigs are available from many specialty food stores or by mail order from Penzey's (see Sources).

Without the addition of the shrimp, the bean salad could be made the day before use. Store, covered and refrigerated. Bring to room temperature before cooking and adding the shrimp.

 THE TRIBECA GRILL COOKBOOK

CRISP FRIED OYSTERS
WITH ASIAN VEGETABLE SLAW AND GARLIC-ANCHOVY AÏOLI

SERVES 6

THIS IS ANOTHER RECIPE THAT HAS STARRED on the Tribeca Grill menu for the entire ten years. From time to time, we have tried to replace it with other oyster preparations, but customers demand the old favorite. I think that its popularity is due to both the presentation and the interesting cross-cultural tastes and textures on the plate—the Asian slaw, the French aïoli, and the crunchy oysters.

30 fresh oysters, shucked, with the shells reserved
2 large eggs
2 tablespoons milk
1 cup Wondra flour (see Note)
2 cups Japanese panko bread crumbs (see Note on
  page 48)
½ cup rock salt
½ cup black sesame seeds
6 fresh banana leaves (see Note)
Asian Vegetable Slaw (recipe follows)
Approximately 6 cups vegetable oil
1 recipe Garlic-Anchovy Aïoli (see page 234)
6 lime wedges

WINE: The wines of Condrieu, made from the aromatic viognier grape, have the texture to stand up to the plumpness of the oysters and the spiciness to match the Asian slaw. A mineral-scented, floral Condrieu by Clusel-Roch or Cuilleron would particularly suit this dish.

1. Line a cookie sheet with parchment paper. Set aside.

2. Wash and drain the oysters. Pat them dry. Wash and dry the shells and set them aside.

3. Whisk together the eggs and milk.

4. Place the Wondra flour into a plastic bag and the panko bread crumbs onto a shallow dish. Working with a few at a time, place the oysters into the Wondra and shake to coat. Dip the oysters into the egg mixture and then into the bread crumbs. Place the coated oysters on the prepared cookie sheet and continue coating until you have prepared all of the oysters. (If not frying immediately, cover and refrigerate.)

5. Combine the rock salt and sesame seeds in a small bowl. Lay a banana leaf out on each of six plates. Place an equal portion of the salt mixture in the center of each leaf. Arrange 5 oyster shells around the banana leaf and fill each one with Asian Vegetable Slaw.

6. Heat the oil to 365°F on a candy thermometer in a deep-fat fryer. Working with a few at a time, drop the breaded oysters into the hot fat and fry for about 1 minute or until golden. Using a slotted spoon, lift the oysters from the fat and drain on paper towel. Continue frying until all of the oysters are cooked.

7. Place a fried oyster on top of each slaw-filled shell. Spoon a small dot of Garlic-Anchovy Aïoli on the top of each oyster. Place a lime wedge next to each oyster and serve.

"Michael Jordan has been a frequent diner at Tribeca. Once, when he discovered that he and Tribeca's general manager, Marty Shapiro, were fellow University of North Carolina alumni and that Marty hadn't been able to find his own pair of size-thirteen Air Jordans (Jordan's size also), he even sent Marty a pair of his own.

"What Michael likes to do best is visit the kitchen. One Saturday night, when the restaurant was jammin', he, Bill Murray, and Dan Aykroyd decided to play some hoops with whatever they could pull from the refrigerators. You can imagine the difficulty the cooks had concentrating on getting the meals off the line with the world's greatest athlete soaring over their heads rebounding a pâté."

ASIAN VEGETABLE SLAW

¼ cup peanut oil
3 tablespoons rice wine vinegar (see Note, page 48)
Juice of 1 lime
Juice of 1 lemon
2 tablespoons soy sauce
1 tablespoon mirin (Japanese rice wine) (see Note, page 48)
1 tablespoon sake (see Note, page 48)
1 tablespoon nam pla (Thai fish sauce) (see Note, page 51)
1 teaspoon sriracha (smooth Thai chili paste) (see Note, page 51)
2 tablespoons sugar
1 teaspoon minced garlic
1 carrot, trimmed, peeled, and julienned
1 leek, trimmed, well washed, and julienned
1 cup shredded bok choy or other cabbage
1 hothouse (seedless) cucumber, well washed, trimmed, and julienned

1. In a medium bowl, whisk together the peanut oil and rice wine vinegar. Add the lime and lemon juices and whisk to combine. Whisk in the soy sauce, mirin, sake, nam pla, and sriracha. When well combined, stir in the sugar and garlic. Set aside.

2. Place the carrot and the leek in boiling salted water for 30 seconds to set the color. Immediately drain and refresh under cold running water until well chilled. Pat dry.

3. Place the blanched carrot and leek in a mixing bowl along with the bok choy and cucumber. Add the reserved sauce and toss to combine. Cover and refrigerate for 2 hours before serving.

NOTE: Wondra flour, a very fine-textured flour, is available in the baking section of most supermarkets.

Banana leaves are available from Asian markets, specialty food stores, and some supermarkets.

Soups, Sandwiches, and Brunches

SOUPS

CHUNKY POTATO-LEEK SOUP WITH ARUGULA PESTO

BUTTERNUT SQUASH AND APPLE SOUP WITH CHESTNUT CREAM

GAZPACHO WITH LOBSTER

WHITE BEAN AND ESCAROLE SOUP WITH DAD'S SAUSAGE BREAD

SPICY CHICKPEA AND TOMATO SOUP

SANDWICHES

ROCK SHRIMP AND CORN FALAFEL WITH TAHINI SAUCE

SOFT-SHELL CRAB SANDWICH WITH AVOCADO AND BEEFSTEAK TOMATOES

GRIDDLED BLACK FOREST HAM AND EMMENTHALER WITH
HORSERADISH CROQUETTES

BREADED EGGPLANT, SMOKED MOZZARELLA, AND BASIL FOCACCIA

BRUNCHES

BANANA-STUFFED FRENCH TOAST

OATMEAL-RAISIN PANCAKES

FRUIT SOUFFLÉ OMELETTE

CHUNKY POTATO-LEEK SOUP WITH ARUGULA PESTO

SERVES 6

THIS IS A SIMPLE, HOMEMADE TYPE of soup with a jolt of flavor from the zesty pesto garnish. I particularly like easy-to-prepare soups that have a lot of texture—where the individual ingredients are evident in the bowl. This is a classic example of the type of soup you will find on the Tribeca Grill menu.

1 head garlic
1 shallot, peeled and chopped
1 tablespoon chopped fresh thyme leaves
1 tablespoon chopped fresh flat-leaf parsley leaves
10 peppercorns
1 bay leaf
1½ tablespoons unsalted butter
1 large onion, peeled and cut into 1-inch dice
1 large leek, white and light-green part only, well washed and cut into 1-inch dice
10 cups Chicken Stock (see page 229) or canned broth
2 large Idaho potatoes, peeled and cut into 1-inch dice
Coarse salt and freshly ground pepper to taste
Arugula Pesto, optional (recipe follows; see Note)

1. Cut the garlic head in half, crosswise. Place it in a cheesecloth bag along with the shallot, thyme, parsley, peppercorns, and bay leaf. Tie the bag closed and set aside.

2. Heat the butter in a large saucepan over medium heat. Add the onion and leek and sauté for about 5 minutes or until the vegetables are translucent. Add the stock or broth and the reserved cheesecloth bag and bring to a boil. Lower the

heat and simmer for 15 minutes. Stir in the potatoes and season to taste with salt and pepper. Bring to a simmer and cook, stirring occasionally, for about 15 minutes or until the potatoes are tender but not mushy. Taste and adjust seasoning with salt and pepper.

3. Remove and discard the cheesecloth bag. Serve hot, either in individual shallow soup bowls or in a soup tureen, garnished, if desired, with a dollop of Arugula Pesto (see Note) in the center.

ARUGULA PESTO

MAKES ABOUT 1½ CUPS

1 bunch of arugula, leaves only, well washed
1 clove garlic, peeled
1 tablespoon freshly grated orange zest
2 tablespoons freshly grated Parmesan cheese
2 tablespoons toasted pine nuts
¾ cup canola oil
Coarse salt and freshly ground pepper to taste

1. Place the arugula leaves in rapidly boiling salted water for 10 seconds to set color. Immediately drain and place under cold running water until well chilled. Pat dry.

2. Place the arugula, garlic, and orange zest in a blender and pulse to combine. Add the cheese and pine nuts and pulse until finely minced. With the motor running, slowly add the oil to make a smooth puree. Taste and adjust the seasoning with salt and pepper. Serve immediately or place in a nonreactive container, cover, and refrigerate for up to 1 day.

NOTE: The Arugula Pesto makes a very tasty garnish for this simple soup, but it is not necessary for its enjoyment. However, if you do take the time to make it, any left over makes a great dressing for pasta or grilled chicken or fish. It can be made up to 24 hours in advance and stored, tightly covered and refrigerated.

Butternut Squash and Apple Soup with Chestnut Cream

SERVES 6

As the seasons change, so do our soups. This is a perfect fall addition to the menu as local squash and apples fill the stands at green markets throughout the city. A hint of spice and apple brandy only adds to its almost sweet, warming goodness. The Chestnut Cream is an elegant garnish, but if you don't have time to make it, just add a small swirl of heavy cream to each bowl before serving.

> *2 medium butternut squash*
> *2 tablespoons olive oil*
> *Coarse salt and freshly ground pepper to taste*
> *⅓ cup unsweetened chestnut puree (see Note)*
> *¼ cup crème fraîche (see Note)*
> *1 teaspoon ground cinnamon*
> *1 teaspoon ground nutmeg*
> *2 tablespoons unsalted butter*
> *3 shallots, peeled and chopped*
> *1 leek, white part only, well washed and chopped*
> *2 tablespoons Calvados or other apple brandy*
> *6 cups Vegetable Stock (see page 230) or canned vegetable broth*
> *2 cups apple juice*
> *3 Granny Smith apples, peeled, cored, and finely chopped*
> *2 star anise*
> *1 bay leaf*
> *½ vanilla bean*

1. Preheat the oven to 375°F.

2. Cut the squash in half lengthwise and remove the seeds. Using a pastry brush, lightly coat the squash with olive oil and season to taste with salt and pepper.

"We are all wildly enthusiastic New York Rangers fans. When they won the Stanley Cup, the Rangers held a victory party at Tribeca. We all got to hold the cup and Drew marched around the restaurant holding it aloft for all to see and touch. What we didn't know was that the coach and general manager were not on speaking terms and we managed to sit them next to each other. But, in the spirit of victory, no harsh words were exchanged and the celebratory dinner went off without a hitch. It showed, once again, how the civility of convivial dining can bring out the best in people."

Place, cut side down, on a cookie sheet in the preheated oven. Bake for about 45 minutes or until the squash is tender when pierced with the point of a sharp knife and the flesh has taken on some color. Remove from the oven and allow to set until cool enough to handle.

3. While the squash is cooling, prepare the Chestnut Cream, if using. Whisk together the chestnut puree and crème fraîche in a small bowl. Cover and refrigerate until ready to use.

4. Scrape the flesh from the squash and place into the bowl of a food processor fitted with the metal blade. Add the cinnamon and nutmeg and process to a smooth puree. Set aside.

5. Heat the butter in a large saucepan over medium heat. Add the shallots and leek and sauté for about 3 minutes or just until the vegetables are beginning to sweat their liquid. Stir in the brandy and cook for about 4 minutes or until the pan is almost dry. Add the broth and juice and bring to a boil. Stir in the apples and the reserved squash puree along with the star anise and bay leaf.

6. Slit the vanilla bean open and scrape its seeds into the soup. (You can keep the vanilla bean and place it in some sugar to add a hint of vanilla for flavoring coffee or tea.) Bring the soup to a boil; lower the heat and simmer, stirring frequently, for about 30 minutes or until the apples are soft. Remove and discard the star anise and bay leaf.

7. Place the soup in a blender and process, in batches if necessary, to a smooth puree. If the soup seems too thick for a smooth, light puree, add additional broth. Taste and adjust seasoning with salt and pepper. (If necessary, transfer to a clean saucepan and reheat over medium heat before serving.)

8. Serve hot, either in individual shallow soup bowls or a large tureen, garnished, if desired, with a dollop of Chestnut Cream in the center.

NOTE: Chestnut puree and crème fraîche are available from specialty food stores. For an elegant presentation, serve the soup in lightly steamed butternut squash halves.

CLOCKWISE FROM TOP RIGHT:
Rock Shrimp and Corn Falafel with Tahini Sauce;
Breaded Eggplant, Smoked Mozzarella, and Basil Focaccia;
Butternut Squash and Apple Soup with Chestnut Cream

GAZPACHO WITH LOBSTER

SERVES 6

THIS IS A SOUP TO CELEBRATE SUMMER, since it should be made only when tomatoes are at their plumpest and sweetest and the peppers and cucumbers are at their most crisp. At its best, this soup is like drinking in summertime. Of course, the soup can stand alone, without the lobster garnish, but it won't be nearly as special. You can also garnish the soup with cooked shrimp, crab or stone crab, or scallops.

> *2 red bell peppers, well washed, cored, seeded, and chopped*
> *2 large, very ripe beefsteak tomatoes, peeled, cored, seeded, and chopped*
> *1 large cucumber, peeled and chopped*
> *1 large red onion, peeled and chopped*
> *¼ cup minced fresh cilantro leaves*
> *6 cups tomato juice*
> *½ cup red wine vinegar*
> *1 teaspoon sriracha (smooth Thai chili paste) (see Note, page 48)*
> *Coarse salt and freshly ground pepper to taste*
> *1 cup finely diced red bell pepper*
> *1 cup finely diced cucumber*
> *½ cup finely diced red onion*
> *½ cup finely diced carrots*
> *½ cup finely diced yellow bell pepper*
> *2 tablespoons fresh lime juice*
> *1½ cups chopped cooked lobster meat*

1. Combine the chopped bell peppers, tomatoes, cucumber, and onion with 2 tablespoons of the cilantro in the bowl of a food processor fitted with the metal blade. Process to a smooth puree. Add the tomato juice, vinegar, and sriracha and process to blend. (This may have to be done in batches.) Season to taste with salt and pepper and pour into a clean, nonreactive container.

THE TRIBECA GRILL COOKBOOK

2. Add the diced red bell pepper, cucumber, onion, carrots, and yellow bell pepper to the puree. Stir in the lime juice. Cover and refrigerate for at least 1 hour to chill thoroughly.

3. When ready to serve, stir in the remaining 2 tablespoons of cilantro. Taste and adjust the seasoning with salt and pepper. Pour equal portions into each of six shallow soup bowls. Garnish the center with lobster and serve well chilled.

NOTE: Either raw or just warmed through, the pureed base for gazpacho also makes a fresh sauce for grilled poultry, fish, or pork. A ring of very thin cucumber slices around the edge of the bowl is an optional garnish.

"In the late eighties and early nineties in New York City, celebrity-owned restaurants were all the rage. Based on my experiences, most of these histrionic echo chambers were big on Hollywood glitter, but when it came to food and service, they were, at best, PG (Pretty Gloomy). So when Robert De Niro's Tribeca Grill opened in 1990, I headed downtown with low expectations.

"Indeed it was a cosmically hip place but my job was eating for *The New York Times*, not stargazing. So, along with my gastronomic dining recruits, I ordered my usual bargeload of dishes to sample. I didn't know much about the chef, Don Pintabona, except that he had a beard. Yet, by the time we had finished our appetizers I had the suspicious feeling that something was wrong at this Hollywood Canteen—the food was very good. I remember trying the startlingly good twist on gazpacho. In my review I wrote: 'If you could distill summer and drink it, the flavor would probably be something like Mr. Pintabona's gazpacho, embellished with chunks of lobster.' Other dishes, memorable for their clean, bright flavors, were equally uplifting.

"I have had the pleasure of watching Don evolve over the years, yet always staying true to his philosophy of uncluttered, full-flavored food. Under his guidance, the restaurant has enjoyed a well-deserved long run. My only complaint is that I never got to meet any of the models who hang out there."

Bryan Miller

WHITE BEAN AND ESCAROLE SOUP WITH DAD'S SAUSAGE BREAD

SERVES 6 TO 8

I THINK THAT I CAN REMEMBER EATING this soup, along with Dad's famous Sausage Bread, in my high chair. I still love it and make it every winter—both at home and in the restaurant. The bread is certainly optional, but if you don't want to make it to serve with the soup, be sure to try it on a cold winter's day. It fills the kitchen with great aromas and is so warm and filling. It always smells like home to me.

> *1 pound dried Great Northern or navy beans*
> *1 clove garlic, peeled*
> *½ teaspoon dried thyme*
> *6 peppercorns*
> *1 bay leaf*
> *½ pound lean bacon, diced*
> *1 small onion, peeled and chopped*
> *1 carrot, peeled, trimmed, and chopped*
> *1 leek, white part only, well washed and chopped*
> *1 stalk celery, chopped*
> *12 cups Chicken Stock (see page 229) or canned chicken broth*
> *Coarse salt and freshly ground pepper to taste*
> *1 tablespoon olive oil*
> *1 teaspoon minced garlic*
> *1 large head escarole, well washed and chopped*
> *Crushed red pepper to taste, optional*
> *Dad's Sausage Bread, optional (recipe follows)*

1. Place the beans in cold water to cover by about 3 inches. Soak for 8 hours or overnight. Drain well and set aside.

2. Combine the whole garlic clove, thyme, peppercorns, and bay leaf in a cheese-cloth bag. Tie the bag closed and set aside.

3. Place the bacon in a large saucepan over medium heat and sauté for about 7 minutes or until the fat has rendered out and the bacon is crisp. Drain off all but 1 tablespoon of the fat. Add the onion, carrot, leek, and celery and sauté for about 5 minutes or until the vegetables are soft but have not taken on any color. Add the reserved soaked beans and cheesecloth bag along with the stock or broth and bring to a boil. Season to taste with salt and pepper. Lower the heat and simmer, stirring frequently, for about 1½ hours or until the beans are very tender.

4. Heat the olive oil in a large sauté pan over medium heat. Add the minced garlic and sauté for 1 minute. Add the escarole and sauté for about 4 minutes or until the escarole is wilted. Add the escarole to the soup. Taste and adjust the seasoning with salt and, if using, crushed red pepper. Serve hot with Dad's Sausage Bread, if desired.

DAD'S SAUSAGE BREAD

MAKES 3 LOAVES

2⅔ cups water
¼ cup olive oil
2 teaspoons honey
8 cups all-purpose flour, plus more as needed
2 packets (7 grams) rapid-rise yeast
1½ tablespoons coarse salt
2 pounds sweet Italian sausage, casing removed, crumbled
2 teaspoons freshly ground pepper
3 large eggs
1 cup finely diced mozzarella cheese
3 tablespoons freshly grated Parmesan cheese
2 tablespoons chopped fresh flat-leaf parsley leaves

1. Heat the water, olive oil, and honey in a small saucepan over low heat to 115°F on a candy thermometer. Set aside and keep warm.

2. Combine the flour, yeast, and salt in a large mixing bowl. Slowly drizzle the water mixture over the flour, blending the liquid in with a wooden spoon. If the dough is too sticky to handle, add additional flour, ¼ cup at a time. Place the dough on a clean surface and knead for about 10 minutes or until very smooth and elastic. Cut the dough into 3 equal pieces and form each piece into a loaf shape. Cover and place in a draft-free spot and allow to rise for about 1 hour or until the loaves have doubled in size.

3. While the dough is rising, place the sausage and pepper in a nonstick sauté pan over medium heat. Cook, stirring frequently, for about 10 minutes or until the sausage is nicely browned. Drain off excess fat; place the sausage on a triple layer of paper towel to drain thoroughly.

4. Place 2 of the eggs in a small bowl and whisk to combine. Set aside. Place the remaining egg in another small bowl and whisk to blend. Set aside.

5. Combine the sausage with the mozzarella and Parmesan cheeses and the parsley. Add the 2 beaten eggs and mix to combine well. Set aside.

6. Cut into but not through each loaf of dough, lengthwise, and open up each half. Place an equal portion of the sausage mixture down the center of each loaf. Pull the sides up and over the sausage to encase it, working the dough closed. Place the loaves, seam side down, on a greased cookie sheet or pizza stone. Cover and let rise for 20 minutes.

7. Preheat the oven to 375°F.

8. Using a pastry brush, lightly coat each loaf with the remaining beaten egg. Place in the preheated oven and bake for about 45 minutes or until golden brown. Remove from the oven and allow to rest for at least 10 minutes before cutting. Serve warm.

NOTE: The soup can be made up to 3 days in advance. Store, covered and refrigerated. Reheat before serving.

SPICY CHICKPEA AND TOMATO SOUP

SERVES 6 TO 8

COLLEEN MCGUIRK, A DEAR FRIEND and a terrific chef, introduced this soup onto the Tribeca Grill fall menu. Although she has since left Tribeca to become director of food and operations for Celebrity Cruises, the soup has been her gift to us. It has great depth of flavor and the fresh tomato, cilantro, and lime bring vibrancy to the rather bland chickpeas. This is truly a gift that keeps on giving!

1 pound dried chickpeas (also called garbanzo beans)
1 head garlic
1 teaspoon dried thyme
10 peppercorns
1 bay leaf
2 tablespoons olive oil
1 large onion, peeled and chopped
1 carrot, peeled, trimmed, and chopped
1 leek, white part only, well washed and chopped
1 stalk celery, chopped
1 teaspoon turmeric
12 cups Chicken Stock (see page 229) or canned chicken broth,
    plus 1 optional cup
Coarse salt and freshly ground pepper to taste
1 tablespoon sriracha (smooth Thai chili paste), or to taste
    (see Note, page 48)
¼ cup garlic slivers
2 cups finely chopped fresh tomatoes
One 16-ounce can chickpeas, well drained
½ cup chopped fresh cilantro leaves
½ cup fresh lime juice

1. Place the dried chickpeas in cold water to cover by at least 3 inches. Allow to soak at least 8 hours or overnight. Drain well and set aside.

2. Cut the garlic head in half, crosswise. Combine it with the thyme, peppercorns, and bay leaf in a cheesecloth bag. Tie the bag closed and set aside.

3. Heat 1 tablespoon of the olive oil in a large saucepan over medium heat. Add the onion, carrot, leek, and celery and sauté for about 5 minutes or until the vegetables are soft but have not taken on any color. Stir in the turmeric. Add the reserved soaked chickpeas and cheesecloth bag along with the stock or broth and bring to a boil. Season to taste with salt and pepper. Lower the heat and add the sriracha. Simmer for about 1½ hours or until the chickpeas are very tender.

4. Heat the remaining olive oil in a medium sauté pan over medium heat. Add the garlic slivers and sauté for about 2 minutes or just until the garlic is golden. (Do not let the garlic get too brown or it will begin to taste burned.) Immediately add the tomatoes to stop the cooking. Add the drained canned chickpeas. Stir in the cilantro and lime juice and season to taste with salt and pepper. (If you would like the soup to have more bite, add a teaspoon of sriracha to the tomato mixture.) Set aside.

5. In batches, place the soup in the bowl of a food processor fitted with the metal blade and process to a smooth puree. Place the puree into a colander and strain into a clean saucepan. If the soup is too thick, add the optional cup of stock. Add the reserved tomato mixture and return to low heat to just reheat. Serve hot.

NOTE: The soup can be made up to 3 days in advance. Store, covered and refrigerated. Reheat before serving.

ROCK SHRIMP AND CORN FALAFEL WITH TAHINI SAUCE

AFTER A CHEF'S TOUR OF ISRAEL, I became wildly enthusiastic about all kinds of Middle Eastern foods. Halvah, chickpeas, yogurt, sesame seeds, eggplant, and pomegranates were just some of the foods that found their place on the Tribeca menu. In Israel, I was also introduced to a falafel mix that I found to be superb. When I returned to New York, I began experimenting with it and developed some new takes on the everyday Israeli street food. Using packaged falafel mix and prepared tahini, this is one of the more interesting and slightly upscale but still convenient versions.

4 ears fresh corn
2 tablespoons unsalted butter
1 large red onion, cut into ¼-inch dice
1 small red bell pepper, cored, seeded, and cut into ¼-inch dice
1 jalapeño chile, seeded and minced, or to taste
1 pound Mira Falafel Mix (see Note)
2 cups water
½ pound cleaned rock shrimp or chopped shrimp
½ cup chopped fresh cilantro leaves
½ cup julienned scallions
Juice of 2 limes
Coarse salt and freshly ground pepper to taste
Approximately 6 cups vegetable oil
24 mini–pita breads
½ pound salad greens, well washed and chopped
½ cup peeled, seeded, and diced tomatoes
Tahini Sauce (recipe follows)

1. Shuck the corn and remove all of the silk. Standing the cob on end and turning the cob as you cut, use a sharp knife to carefully remove the kernels from the cob. Discard the cobs (see Note) and set the kernels aside.

2. Heat the butter in a large sauté pan over medium heat. Add the onion, bell pepper, jalapeño, and the reserved corn kernels and cook, stirring frequently, for about 5 minutes or until the vegetables are just crisp-tender. Remove from the heat and set aside to cool.

3. Combine the falafel mix and water in a large mixing bowl. When well blended, set aside to rest for 10 minutes.

4. Stir the reserved corn mixture into the falafel mix. Add the shrimp, cilantro, and scallions, and mix to just combine. Stir in the lime juice and adjust the seasoning with salt and pepper to taste.

5. Shape the falafel mixture into 1-inch balls.

6. Heat the oil to 350°F in a deep-fat fryer (or deep saucepan) over high heat. Add the falafel balls, a few at a time, and fry until golden brown. Remove from the oil and drain on a double thickness of paper towel. Continue frying until all of the falafels are cooked.

7. Slice open each pita. Stuff 1 falafel into each pita. Nestle a few pieces of salad greens into each pocket and sprinkle a bit of diced tomato over the greens. Drizzle Tahini Sauce into the pocket and serve immediately.

TAHINI SAUCE

¼ cup cold water
¼ cup fresh cilantro leaves, tightly packed
1 cup Sahadi Tahini Sauce (see Note)
1 cup plain yogurt
½ cup crème fraîche (see Note, page 108)
Juice of 1 lime
2 tablespoons olive oil
Coarse salt and freshly ground pepper to taste

1. Pour the water into a blender. Add the cilantro and process to a smooth liquid.

2. Place the Tahini Sauce, yogurt, crème fraîche, and lime juice into a small mixing bowl. Stir in the cilantro puree along with the olive oil, blending well. Taste and adjust the seasoning with salt and pepper to taste. Store, covered and refrigerated, until ready to use.

NOTE: Mira Falafel Mix and Sahadi Tahini Sauce are available from specialty food stores, many Middle Eastern groceries, or by mail order from Kalustyan Orient Export Trading Corporation (see Sources). If you cannot locate these brands, you may substitute any other high-quality brand of either product.

Scraped corncobs make an excellent stock for vegetable, chicken, or fish soups and can also be used to add additional flavor to canned chicken broth.

SOFT-SHELL CRAB SANDWICH WITH AVOCADO AND BEEFSTEAK TOMATOES

SERVES 6

TO ME, THERE IS NO SANDWICH BETTER than one filled with a crisp soft-shell crab. And forget about health issues, the crab has to be fried. Combine the crispy crab with a nice soft roll, a few slices of creamy avocado, ripe Jersey tomatoes, and you have heaven on earth. These are always on our menu in the late spring and early summer, when soft-shells are at their best.

½ cup Garlic-Anchovy Aïoli (see page 234)
1 tablespoon finely chopped dill pickles, well drained
3 large eggs
2 tablespoons milk
1 cup Wondra flour (see Note, page 69)
1 cup Japanese panko bread crumbs (see Note, page 48)
3 avocados
Juice of 1 lime
½ teaspoon cayenne pepper
Pinch of ground coriander
Coarse salt and freshly ground pepper to taste
6 soft-shell crabs, well cleaned, rinsed, and patted dry
Approximately 6 cups vegetable oil
6 large, soft rolls, preferably potato rolls
6 slices red beefsteak tomato
6 slices yellow beefsteak tomato
1 bunch of arugula, leaves only, well washed and dried

1. Combine the aïoli and pickles in a small bowl. Cover and refrigerate until ready to use.

2. Place the eggs in a shallow bowl and whisk in the milk until very well combined. Set aside.

3. Place the Wondra in a shallow bowl and the bread crumbs in a resealable plastic bag. Set aside.

4. Cut the avocados in half lengthwise. Remove the pit and peel each half. Cut each half into 6 thin slices, cutting down to but not through the thicker bottom half. Fan the 6 slices out and sprinkle with lime juice to keep the avocado from discoloring. Set aside.

5. Combine the cayenne and coriander with salt and pepper to taste and generously season the crabs with the mixture. Place the crabs in the Wondra, turning to coat both sides. Dip each crab into the egg mixture and then place them in the bag of bread crumbs and toss to coat well.

6. Pour 2 inches of oil into a deep skillet. Place over high heat and bring to 350°F on a candy thermometer. Add the coated crabs, a couple at a time, and fry, turning once, for about 4 minutes or until golden brown. Drain on paper towel.

7. Cut the rolls in half lengthwise. Spread the top half with the reserved aïoli. Place a red and a yellow tomato slice on the bottom half. Top the tomatoes with some arugula leaves and a fanned-out avocado half. Lay a soft-shell crab on top and cover with the top half of the roll. Cut in half and serve immediately.

 THE TRIBECA GRILL COOKBOOK

GRIDDLED BLACK FOREST HAM AND EMMENTHALER WITH HORSERADISH CROQUETTES

SERVES 6

NOTHING COULD BE MORE STRAIGHTFORWARD than a classic ham and cheese sandwich, so why fool with perfection? At Tribeca, we just give it a little tweak and garnish the plate with Horseradish Croquettes rather than potato chips. If time is of the essence, don't worry about making the croquettes.

> *1 cup grainy mustard*
> *¼ cup honey*
> *12 slices sourdough bread*
> *1¼ pounds Black Forest ham, thinly sliced*
> *1¼ pounds Emmenthaler cheese, thinly sliced*
> *¼ cup (½ stick) unsalted butter, softened*
> *18 Horseradish Croquettes, optional (recipe follows)*

1. Preheat the oven to 350°F.

2. Combine the mustard and honey in a small bowl. Spread the mustard mixture on one side of each slice of bread. Place about 3 ounces each of ham and cheese on the mustard-coated side of 6 slices of bread. Cover with the remaining slices of bread, mustard-coated side on top of the ham and cheese, and pat down to push the sandwich together. Lightly coat the outside of the sandwiches with the softened butter.

3. Heat a nonstick griddle over medium-high heat. Add the sandwiches, in batches if necessary, and cook for about 3 minutes or until golden. Turn and cook the remaining side until nicely browned.

"**H**arvey Weinstein, one of our investors and the head of Miramax Films, was forever ordering a ham and cheese sandwich. Since we didn't have such a simple sandwich on the menu, we would have to run across the street to our local deli to buy one. Finally, after many, many trips to the deli, we wised up and put our version of a ham and cheese sandwich on the menu. Now that it is one of the biggest hits on the lunch menu, Harvey no longer has to call out for 'a quick ham and cheese.'"

4. Place the browned sandwiches on a cookie sheet in the preheated oven and bake for about 6 minutes or until the cheese is melted. Remove from the oven and cut into triangles. Serve hot with Horseradish Croquettes, if desired.

HORSERADISH CROQUETTES

MAKES ABOUT 18

4 cups Whipped Potatoes (see page 183)
½ cup freshly grated horseradish or ¼ cup well-drained
*   prepared horseradish*
Coarse salt and freshly ground pepper to taste
3 large eggs
2 tablespoons milk
1 cup Wondra flour (see Note, page 69)
1 cup Italian-seasoned bread crumbs
Approximately 4 cups vegetable oil

1. Place the potatoes in a mixing bowl and beat in the horseradish. Season to taste with salt and pepper. Shape the potato mixture into 2-inch round balls and set aside.

2. Place the eggs in a shallow bowl and whisk in the milk until well combined. Place the flour in a shallow bowl and the seasoned bread crumbs in another shallow bowl. Place the bowls in a line—flour, eggs, and bread crumbs. Roll each croquette in the flour, then the egg mixture, and finally the bread crumbs.

3. Heat the oil to 375°F on a candy thermometer in a deep saucepan or deep-fat fryer. Add the croquettes, a few at a time, and fry for about 3 minutes or until golden brown. Using a slotted spoon, remove the croquettes from the oil and drain on paper towel. Season to taste with salt and pepper and serve hot.

Griddled Black Forest Ham and Emmenthaler
and Chunky Potato-Leek Soup with Arugula Pesto

Breaded Eggplant, Smoked Mozzarella, and Basil Focaccia

SERVES 6

THIS IS THE TRIBECA GRILL VERSION of a veggie sandwich. You have to forgo some health concerns because the fried eggplant is the best, *but* if fat is a problem in your diet, you can grill or roast the eggplant with very tasty results. The focaccia makes the sandwich, but if you can't find it or don't want to make it, use a good crusty peasant bread.

> *1 bunch of fresh basil, leaves only, well washed*
> *2 cloves garlic, chopped*
> *¼ cup freshly grated Parmesan cheese*
> *¼ cup toasted pine nuts*
> *1½ cups canola oil*
> *Coarse salt and freshly ground pepper to taste*
> *5 large eggs*
> *2 tablespoons milk*
> *2 cups Wondra flour (see Note, page 69)*
> *3 cups Italian-seasoned bread crumbs*
> *1 large eggplant, trimmed*
> *Approximately 4 cups vegetable oil*
> *1 large rosemary focaccia, about 12 inches by 9 inches*
> *2 cups Roasted Red Peppers (see page 238)*
> *2 cups Oven-Dried Tomatoes (see page 238)*
> *1 pound smoked mozzarella, thinly sliced*
> *½ cup Tomato Oil (see page 236)*

1. Place the basil in rapidly boiling salted water for 10 seconds. Immediately drain and place under cold running water until well chilled. Pat dry.

2. Place the basil and garlic in a blender and begin to puree. Add the Parmesan and pine nuts and process until almost smooth. With the motor running, slowly add the canola oil and process until smooth. Season to taste with salt and pepper. Set aside.

3. Place the eggs and milk in a shallow bowl and whisk until well combined. Place the flour in a shallow bowl and the seasoned bread crumbs in another shallow bowl. Place the bowls in a line—flour, eggs, and bread crumbs.

4. Cut the eggplant, lengthwise, into very thin slices on a slicing machine or with a Japanese vegetable slicer (see page 19) or carefully by hand. Dip the slices into the flour; then the egg mixture and finally the bread crumbs. Season with salt and pepper to taste.

5. Heat ¼ inch of vegetable oil to 350°F on a candy thermometer in a large, deep skillet. Add the breaded eggplant, a few slices at a time, and fry for about 1 minute or until the eggplant is golden. Carefully lift the eggplant from the oil and drain on a triple layer of paper towel.

6. Preheat the oven to 350°F.

7. Using a bread knife, cut the focaccia in half, lengthwise. Lay the warm eggplant on the cut side of the bottom half to fully cover it. Cover the eggplant with a layer of roasted peppers. Cover the peppers with a layer of tomatoes. Place the smoked mozzarella over all.

8. Spread some of the reserved basil pesto over the cut side of the top half of the focaccia. Drizzle Tomato Oil over the pesto and place the top half onto the bottom.

9. Cut the focaccia into 6 equal pieces. Place the pieces on a cookie sheet in the preheated oven and bake for about 10 minutes or until the cheese has melted and the sandwiches are hot. Serve immediately with a salad, fries, or potato chips, if desired.

Banana-Stuffed French Toast

Serves 6

THIS LONGTIME BRUNCH FAVORITE was recently featured on the Food Network's *Cooking Live* with Sara Moulton when she requested an easy-to-prepare but unusual breakfast or brunch dish. Not only is this dish easy to prepare, much of the preparation can be done in advance, which makes it perfect for a Sunday football brunch.

> *½ cup (1 stick) unsalted butter*
> *¼ cup maple syrup*
> *Two 6-inch-long loaves of brioche, challah,*
> *   or other slightly sweet egg bread*
> *2 to 3 ripe, firm whole bananas, peeled*
> *8 large eggs*
> *2 very ripe bananas, chopped*
> *2 cups heavy cream*
> *1 teaspoon sugar*
> *1 teaspoon ground cinnamon*
> *½ teaspoon ground nutmeg*
> *1 teaspoon pure vanilla extract*
> *Approximately 2 tablespoons canola oil*

1. Combine the butter and maple syrup in the bowl of a food processor fitted with the metal blade. Process until very smooth. Scrape the maple butter into a serving bowl and set aside.

2. Trim and discard the ends from each loaf of bread. Using a long, narrow object (such as a sharpening steel or a wooden spoon handle), pierce a hole through the center of each loaf of bread, pushing out slightly to make the hole large

5. Using an electric mixer, beat the egg yolks with the remaining sugar until very light and fluffy. Fold in the vanilla and lemon zest. When well blended, fold in the beaten egg whites.

6. Pour the melted butter into a 7-inch, ovenproof omelette pan over medium heat. Place the fruit (if sliced, fan it out) into the pan and pour in the batter to cover the fruit. Cook for 1½ minutes. Place in the preheated oven and bake for about 10 minutes or until the omelette is puffed and golden.

7. Remove from the oven and carefully invert onto a serving plate. Dust with confectioners' sugar and serve.

NOTE: If desired, you can garnish the plate with fresh fruit and mint.

Pasta

and Risotto

ANGEL HAIR PASTA WITH ROASTED PLUM TOMATOES

FARFALLE WITH DUCK, WILD MUSHROOMS, AND ROSEMARY CREAM SAUCE

SWEET PEA RAVIOLI WITH WILD MUSHROOMS AND SWEET PEA BROTH

BEET GNOCCHI WITH BRAISED OXTAIL AND HORSERADISH SAUCE

CREAMY LEMON AND HERB RISOTTO WITH LOBSTER

WATERCRESS RISOTTO WITH NANTUCKET BAY SCALLOPS

RISOTTO OF THAI BLACK RICE

1½ tablespoons minced fresh flat-leaf parsley leaves
2 tablespoons finely diced celery, blanched
2 tablespoons finely diced carrot, blanched
2 tablespoons finely diced leek, blanched
Freshly grated Parmesan cheese to taste, optional

1. Heat 2 tablespoons of the butter in a large saucepan over medium heat. Add the chopped shallots and garlic and sauté for about 4 minutes or until very soft but not colored. Raise the heat and add the brandy. Bring to a boil and boil for 1 minute. Add the wine and, again, bring to a boil. Lower the heat and simmer for about 15 minutes or until the liquid is reduced by one half. Add the stock or broth, peppercorns, 1 rosemary sprig, and the bay leaf. Raise the heat and bring to a boil. Lower the heat and simmer for about 20 minutes or until the liquid is reduced by one half. Season to taste with salt and white pepper.

2. While the broth is reducing, place the cream and 1 of the remaining rosemary sprigs in a small, heavy saucepan over medium heat. Bring to a simmer. Lower the heat and gently simmer for about 12 minutes or until the cream is reduced by one half. Watch carefully to insure that the cream does not boil over. Season to taste with salt and white pepper.

3. Whisk the reduced cream into the reduced broth. Remove from the heat and strain through a fine sieve into the top half of a double boiler (or, if making in advance of use, into a clean container with a lid). Taste and, if necessary, adjust the seasoning with salt and white pepper. Place over hot water, cover loosely, and keep warm.

4. Bring about 4 quarts of salted water to boil in a large saucepan or pasta pot over high heat. Add the farfalle and boil, stirring frequently, for about 12 minutes or until the pasta is al dente. Drain well.

5. While the pasta is cooking, heat the olive oil in a large sauté pan over medium heat. Add the minced garlic and sauté for 2 minutes. Stir in the mushrooms and salt and black pepper to taste and sauté for about 15 minutes or until the mushrooms have exuded most of their liquid and are quite tender. Stir in the Duck Confit and the remaining 1 tablespoon butter and cook for about 2 minutes or until the mixture is hot. Taste and adjust the seasoning with salt and

black pepper. Toss in the parsley; then, the diced celery, carrot, and leek. Taste and adjust the seasoning with salt and pepper and, if desired, up to 2 tablespoons of additional butter.

6. Toss the drained pasta with the mushroom mixture. Ladle about ¼ cup of the cream sauce into each of six shallow pasta bowls. Top the sauce with the pasta and sprinkle grated cheese over all. Garnish with a fresh rosemary sprig and serve.

"On a freezing cold Saturday in January of 1990, I stood with my partners, Robert De Niro, Christopher Walken, Lou Diamond Phillips, and a few other investors, in the now-defunct Martinson's Coffee building. Although all of the contracts had not yet been signed, we had, at Drew's behest, purchased a huge bar at the Maxwell's Plum auction (Maxwell's Plum being a hugely successful Upper East Side restaurant whose time had come and gone) to be the centerpiece of our about-to-be restaurant.

"There we stood, freezing, in the unheated former warehouse which we hoped would be opening soon under the name Tribeca Grill. We all became designers of the moment. We had made a huge cardboard mock-up of the bar which was standing in the middle of this vast empty space. Together, we would gingerly lift the cardboard to try it in different locations around the room. Moving back and forth and taking tiny steps, we must have looked like a flock of penguins looking for a spot to nest.

"Finally, we all settled on *the best* location—in the center of the room with a view of the doorway and plenty of space all around to let drinkers comfortably schmooze as they waited (we hoped) for their table. I'll never forget that moment. We had all taken time on a cold winter morning to help make the restaurant work. This was not just an investment of cash, we were able to make a creative contribution, also. I think that a little bit of our spirit and soul remained in the space that day. In fact, I can still feel it every time I walk in."

Stewart Lane

THE TRIBECA GRILL COOKBOOK

Sweet Pea Ravioli with Wild Mushrooms and Sweet Pea Broth

SERVES 6

I LOVE TO MAKE UNUSUAL RAVIOLIS. With the first sign of spring, I will often use sweet, tender green peas to create one of my favorite vegetable-flavored pasta fillings. The filling and the broth work together to make an extraordinary, light pasta main course that almost sings of springtime. Plus, the cheese mixture is a great base for any other vegetable flavoring.

1 tablespoon olive oil
3 shallots, peeled and minced
1 1/2 teaspoons minced garlic
3 cups shelled fresh peas, blanched, or frozen petit peas, thawed
2 tablespoons chopped fresh mint leaves
1/2 cup plus 2 tablespoons freshly grated Parmesan cheese
1/2 cup mascarpone cheese (see Note)
1/2 cup ricotta cheese
Coarse salt and freshly ground pepper to taste
Approximately 1/4 cup cornmeal
1 large egg
Pasta Dough (see page 241)
3/4 cup Vegetable Stock (see page 230) or canned broth
5 tablespoons unsalted butter, softened
1 cup thinly sliced oyster mushrooms (see Note)
1 cup thinly sliced shiitake mushrooms (see Note)
2 tablespoons minced fresh chives

WINE: The aggressive, herbaceous, crisp style of Sauvignon Blanc, particularly one like Cloudy Bay from New Zealand, pairs well with the vegetable mixture.

1. Heat the olive oil in a medium sauté pan over medium heat. Add the shallots and 1 teaspoon of the garlic and sauté for 4 minutes. Remove from the heat and allow to cool.

2. Place 2 cups of the peas and the mint in the bowl of a food processor fitted with the metal blade. Process to combine. Add 2 tablespoons of the Parmesan cheese, the mascarpone and ricotta cheeses, and salt and pepper to taste. Process until quite smooth.

3. Lightly coat a baking sheet or platter with the cornmeal.

4. Whisk the egg with 1 tablespoon of cold water. Set aside.

5. Cut the Pasta Dough into 2-inch-wide strips.

6. Place a tablespoon of the pea-cheese mixture at 2-inch intervals down some of the strips to make 34 mounds. Using a pastry brush, lightly coat the edges of the strips and the spaces between the mounds with the reserved egg wash. Loosely place a strip of dough over each mounded strip and press down between the mounds and along the edges to seal the strips together. Using a fluted pastry cutter, cut around each mound to form 34 ravioli. Place the ravioli on the prepared baking sheet or platter. Cover lightly with plastic wrap and refrigerate until ready to use (see Note).

7. Combine the remaining 1 cup of peas with the Vegetable Stock in a blender and process until smooth. Pour into a clean saucepan and season to taste with salt and pepper. Set aside.

8. Heat 1 tablespoon of the butter in a medium sauté pan over medium heat. Add the remaining ½ teaspoon garlic and sauté for 1 minute. Stir in the mushrooms and sauté for about 3 minutes or until the mushrooms have exuded some liquid and are softening. Season to taste with salt and pepper and set aside.

9. Place the pea broth over low heat. When hot, whisk in 2 tablespoons of the butter. Keep on low heat.

10. Bring about 4 quarts of salted water to boil in a large saucepan or pasta pot over high heat. Add the ravioli and cook for about 3 minutes or until the water returns

to a rapid boil and the ravioli are floating on top. Using a slotted spoon, lift the ravioli from the water and place in a colander to drain. Transfer to a mixing bowl and toss with 2 tablespoons of the butter and salt and pepper to taste.

11. Ladle warm pea broth into each of six shallow pasta bowls. Place 5 ravioli around the edge of the bowl in the broth. Spoon some mushrooms into the center of the bowl. Sprinkle chives and the remaining Parmesan over the top. Serve immediately.

NOTE: The ravioli can be stored, covered and refrigerated, for up to 2 days or frozen for up to 6 months. If frozen, they will take a bit longer to cook.

Most mushrooms that were once only gathered in the wild are now cultivated, but they are still most frequently referred to as "wild." In this recipe, you can, in fact, use any combination of "wild" or cultivated mushrooms including just plain button mushrooms if that is what is available to you.

Mascarpone cheese is available at Italian markets, specialty food stores, and some supermarkets.

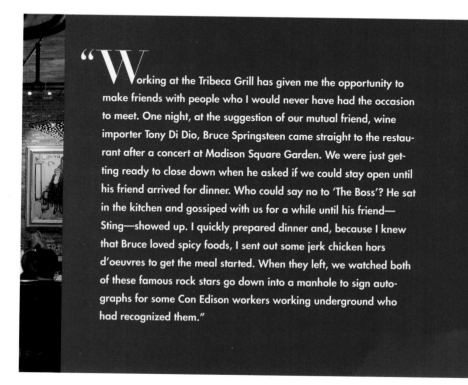

"Working at the Tribeca Grill has given me the opportunity to make friends with people who I would never have had the occasion to meet. One night, at the suggestion of our mutual friend, wine importer Tony Di Dio, Bruce Springsteen came straight to the restaurant after a concert at Madison Square Garden. We were just getting ready to close down when he asked if we could stay open until his friend arrived for dinner. Who could say no to 'The Boss'? He sat in the kitchen and gossiped with us for a while until his friend—Sting—showed up. I quickly prepared dinner and, because I knew that Bruce loved spicy foods, I sent out some jerk chicken hors d'oeuvres to get the meal started. When they left, we watched both of these famous rock stars go down into a manhole to sign autographs for some Con Edison workers working underground who had recognized them."

Beet Gnocchi with Braised Oxtail and Horseradish Sauce

SERVES 6

I DO MANY, MANY TYPES of gnocchi throughout the year, often utilizing a seasonal vegetable to heighten their freshness. In this instance, beets, oxtail, and horseradish come together to make a fall entrée. However, these light little dumplings can also be served as an appetizer or, without the added richness of the braised oxtail and cream, they would also be a standout side dish.

2 large (about 1½ pounds) Idaho potatoes, peeled and
    coarsely chopped
2 large (about 1¼ pounds) red beets, peeled and
    coarsely chopped
1 large egg
Approximately 3 cups all-purpose flour
¼ cup freshly grated Parmesan cheese
1 teaspoon coarse salt, plus more to taste
½ teaspoon freshly ground black pepper, plus more to taste
1 cup dry white wine
5 large shallots, peeled and chopped
8 large cloves garlic, peeled and chopped
½ cup chopped leeks, white part only
10 peppercorns
5 sprigs of fresh thyme
1 bay leaf
4 cups heavy cream
¼ cup freshly grated horseradish
2 tablespoons unsalted butter
3 cups Braised Oxtails (see page 241)
½ cup freshly grated Parmesan cheese

WINE: The body, sweetness, and spice necessary to stand up to this robust dish can be found in a full-bodied, blackberry- and pepper-flavored Zinfandel like that produced by Ravenswood's single vineyard, Monte Rosso in Sonoma.

1. Combine the potatoes and beets in a large saucepan of cold, salted water to cover over high heat. Bring to a boil. Lower the heat and simmer for 20 minutes or until very tender. Drain well.

2. Preheat the oven to 200°F or the lowest setting.

3. Push the potatoes and beets through a food mill or potato ricer. Place the riced mixture on a baking sheet with sides in the preheated oven and bake, occasionally turning the mixture, for about 1 hour or until the mixture is quite dry. Remove from the oven and allow to come to room temperature. Cover with plastic wrap and refrigerate for about 30 minutes or until chilled slightly.

4. Scrape the potato-beet mixture into a mixing bowl. Beat in the egg. When well combined, beat in 2½ cups of the flour along with the cheese, 1 teaspoon of salt, and ½ teaspoon of pepper. If necessary, add the additional flour to make a soft dough. When a soft dough has formed, using your hands, knead the dough for about 4 minutes. Form it into a ball and cover with plastic wrap. Set aside to rest for at least 2 hours but no more than 8 hours.

5. Line two baking sheets with parchment paper. Set aside.

6. Bring a large saucepan or pasta pot of salted water to boil over high heat.

7. Divide the dough into 4 equal parts. Roll each piece into a long, thin strip about ½ inch in diameter. Cut each strip into ¼-inch pieces. Drop the gnocchi by the handful into the boiling salted water. Cook for about 3 minutes or until the gnocchi rise to the top. Using a slotted spoon, lift the gnocchi from the water and place them in ice water to stop the cooking. Again, using the slotted spoon, lift the gnocchi from the ice water and place them on the prepared baking sheets. Continue boiling and cooling gnocchi until all are cooked. Cover the cooked gnocchi with a damp towel (see Note).

8. Combine the wine, shallots, garlic, leeks, peppercorns, thyme, and bay leaf in a large saucepan over medium-high heat. Bring to a boil. Lower the heat and simmer for 5 minutes or until the wine has reduced by one quarter.

9. Raise the heat and add the cream. Bring to a bare simmer, taking care not to let the cream boil over. Lower the heat and simmer for about 20 minutes or until the cream has reduced by one half. Remove from the heat and strain the

THE TRIBECA GRILL COOKBOOK

sauce through a fine sieve into the top half of a double boiler. Whisk in the horseradish and season to taste with salt and pepper. Place over very hot water and keep warm.

10. Heat the butter in a large sauté pan over medium heat. Add the gnocchi and oxtails and toss to combine. Season to taste with salt and pepper and keep tossing until the mixture is very hot. Pour the sauce over the mixture and toss to combine.

11. Place equal portions of the gnocchi in each of six shallow pasta bowls. Sprinkle Parmesan cheese over the top and serve.

NOTE: Gnocchi can be stored, covered with a damp towel, for up to 3 days in the refrigerator or placed in resealable plastic bags, labeled, and frozen for up to 6 months.

CREAMY LEMON AND HERB RISOTTO WITH LOBSTER

SERVES 6

WE ALWAYS HAVE RISOTTO on the menu at Tribeca, so I am forever looking for inspiration to spruce up a rather straightforward homey dish. This recipe couldn't be less homey with the addition of the luxurious, sweet, lobster garnish. Just a hint of lemon adds a fresh breeze and boosts the creaminess out of the ordinary. If you don't poach the lobsters at home, use a mixture of equal parts clam broth, chicken broth, and water to cook the risotto. You will probably need about 8 cups. Also know that the risotto is absolutely wonderful without the lobster garnish.

4 cups Court Bouillon (see page 231)
Three 1½-pound lobsters
½ cup (1 stick) unsalted butter, plus more to taste, at
  room temperature
1 cup finely diced onion
1 cup dry white wine
2 cups Arborio rice
2 tablespoons fresh lemon juice
Freshly grated zest of 2 lemons
2 tablespoons finely diced celery, blanched
2 tablespoons finely diced carrot, blanched
2 tablespoons finely diced leek, blanched
Coarse salt and freshly ground white pepper to taste
3 tablespoons unsalted butter, melted
3 tablespoons chopped fresh flat-leaf parsley, chives,
  or tarragon leaves

WINE: A classic, full-bodied white Burgundy, such as Lafon Meursault Charmes, could well match the richness and extravagance of the risotto.

1. Bring the Court Bouillon to a boil in a stockpot over high heat. Add the lobsters and lower the heat. Simmer for 5 minutes. Lift the lobsters from the boiling liquid and carefully remove the tails and the claws. Place the claws and bodies back into the bouillon and boil for an additional 4 minutes. Lift the claws from the pot, keeping the liquid on low heat at a bare simmer.

2. Remove the meat from the tail and claws of the lobster, keeping the pieces intact. Cut the tails in half, lengthwise. Place the meat in a small roasting pan and set aside.

3. Heat 1 tablespoon of the room-temperature butter in a large, heavy-bottomed saucepan over medium heat. Add the onion and sauté for about 4 minutes or until the onion is soft but has not taken on any color. Add the wine and cook, stirring occasionally, for about 10 minutes or until the liquid has almost evaporated.

4. Preheat the broiler.

5. Stir the rice into the onion and sauté for about 2 minutes or until the rice is slightly toasted. Immediately add 1 cup of the hot Court Bouillon, or enough to just cover the rice. Cook, stirring constantly and adding Court Bouillon, 1 cup at a time as the liquid is absorbed by the rice, for about 25 minutes, or until the rice is beginning to be creamy but is still firm to the tooth. Add the lemon juice, two thirds of the zest, and the remaining room-temperature butter and stir to combine. Fold in the celery, carrot, and leek and season to taste with salt and pepper. Allow to rest for 5 minutes.

6. Drizzle the melted butter over the reserved lobster meat. Season to taste with salt and pepper and place under the broiler for 2 minutes.

7. If desired, beat additional room-temperature butter into the risotto just before serving. Spoon the risotto into six shallow pasta bowls. Place one half of a lobster tail and one claw in the center of each bowl. Sprinkle the herbs and remaining lemon zest over the top and serve.

OVERLEAF (CLOCKWISE FROM BOTTOM LEFT):
Creamy Lemon and Herb Risotto with Lobster, Risotto of Thai Black Rice, Watercress Risotto with Nantucket Bay Scallops

vegetables have softened. Add the curry paste and stir to combine. Add the coconut milk and heavy cream and bring to a boil. Add reserved basil stems along with the lime leaves, nam pla, and honey. Season to taste with salt and pepper. Cook, stirring frequently, for about 10 minutes or until the sauce has reduced by one half and has thickened slightly. Remove from the heat and strain through a fine sieve into the top half of a double boiler over very hot water (see Note). Cover lightly and keep warm.

3. Preheat the oven to 375°F.

4. Place the Vegetable Stock or broth in a medium saucepan over medium heat. Bring to a simmer; immediately lower the heat to just keep the liquid hot.

5. Heat the peanut oil in a medium, heavy-bottomed, ovenproof saucepan. Add the remaining shallots and garlic and sauté for 3 minutes. Add the sake and cook, stirring frequently, for about 10 minutes or until the liquid has almost evaporated. Add the rice and sauté for 1 minute or until the rice is slightly toasted. Pour the hot Vegetable Stock over the rice to cover it by 2 inches. Add the bell pepper and salt and pepper to taste and stir to combine. Cover and place in the preheated oven and bake for about 12 minutes or until all of the liquid has been absorbed by the rice. Remove the rice from the oven. Add the cilantro and toss to just combine. Taste and, if necessary, adjust the seasoning with salt and pepper. Keep covered and set aside.

6. Ladle about ⅓ cup of sauce into each of six shallow pasta bowls. Spoon some of the risotto over the sauce and sprinkle with garlic chives and the reserved basil chiffonade.

NOTE: Thai purple basil, Thai green curry paste, Kaffir lime leaves, nam pla (Thai fish sauce), and Thai black or purple rice are available from Asian markets and some specialty food stores.

Score the back of Kaffir lime leaves with a knife before slicing them. This helps release their fragrance. If you can't find them, replace the 2 leaves with 1 teaspoon fresh lime juice.

The Green Curry Sauce can be made up to 3 days in advance and stored, covered and refrigerated. Reheat in a double boiler when ready to use.

Seafood

BROOK TROUT with PECANS, LEMON, and PARSLEY BROWN BUTTER

GRILLED BLACK BASS with ROSEMARY, FENNEL, and CURED LEMONS

CRAB-CRUSTED SEA BASS with BRAISED ENDIVE, PINE NUT POLENTA, and RED WINE FUMET

SPICE-RUBBED YELLOWFIN TUNA with SEAWEED SALAD

BARBECUE-GLAZED SALMON with BONIATO PUREE and CHILI-CITRUS VINAIGRETTE

PAN-SEARED SNAPPER with TOASTED COUSCOUS

PAELLA QUISBERT

SPICY MUSSELS with BABY BOK CHOY

Brook Trout with Pecans, Lemon, and Parsley Brown Butter

SERVES 6

THIS IS ALMOST A CLASSIC FRENCH preparation with just the hint of Italian seasonings in the bread crumbs taking it out of the norm. Although the recipe calls for peanut oil, if your diet allows, the fish is most delicious sautéed in clarified butter. Served with some roasted baby vegetables, you have a plate fit for a time-honored bistro "plat du jour."

2 lemons
1½ cups plus 2 tablespoons finely chopped pecans
1½ cups Italian-seasoned bread crumbs
¾ cup chopped fresh flat-leaf parsley leaves
Six 10-ounce brook trout, cleaned and boned
    with head and tail removed
Coarse salt and freshly ground pepper to taste
½ cup peanut oil
1 cup (2 sticks) unsalted butter

WINE: A toasty Chardonnay like Flowers Camp Meeting Ridge or Peter Michael Mon Plaisir has the elegance, length, and citrus component to work well with the flavors in this dish.

1. Zest and juice both lemons, separately reserving the zest and the juice. Set aside.

2. Combine 1½ cups of the pecans with the bread crumbs and ¼ cup of the parsley on a large plate.

3. Open up and cut the trout, diagonally, into two fillets. Season both the flesh and skin sides with salt and pepper to taste and then, working with one at a time, press the flesh side of the trout into the pecan mixture to make a thin coating.

4. Preheat the oven to 375°F.

5. Using 2 tablespoons of the peanut oil, generously grease a baking sheet. Set aside.

6. Heat 3 tablespoons of oil in a large sauté pan over high heat. When very hot but not smoking, add 6 trout fillets and sear to set the crust. Turn and sear the other side. Using a fish spatula or a large, wide spatula, transfer the trout to the prepared baking sheet. Add additional oil to the pan and continue to sear the remaining trout. When seared, transfer to the prepared baking sheet.

7. Place the baking sheet in the preheated oven and bake the trout for about 7 minutes or until cooked through.

8. While the trout is baking, melt the butter in a nonstick sauté pan over medium-high heat. Watching carefully and lowering the heat if necessary, allow the butter to foam and turn golden brown. Immediately add the lemon juice and salt and pepper to taste. While the butter is still foaming, add the remaining pecans and parsley. Do not allow the butter to burn or it will be unusable.

9. Place 2 fillets on each of six dinner plates and pour the Parsley Brown Butter over the top. Sprinkle with the reserved lemon zest and serve.

NOTE: A nice assortment of spring or baby vegetables can serve as an optional garnish.

Grilled Black Bass with Rosemary, Fennel, and Cured Lemons

Serves 6

When I visit my relatives in Sicily, we often gather at their vacation house in the hills above Palermo. On one of my first trips, my grandmother's sister prepared some local bass that she marinated and then grilled on an open fire, all the while brushing the fish with branches of wild rosemary she had just pulled from the earth. I don't think that I had ever experienced flavors so direct and pure and, from the memory of them, I created this homage to Sicilian cooks.

3 fennel bulbs
3 large shallots, peeled and chopped
3 large cloves garlic, peeled and chopped
6 sprigs of fresh rosemary
1 cup olive oil
1 cup anisette (see Note)
Three 2¼-pound black bass, cleaned
with head and tail intact
Coarse salt and freshly ground pepper to taste
12 slices fresh lemon
1 tablespoon fennel seeds
3 bay leaves
¾ cup julienned fresh basil
1 cup Cured Lemons (see page 237)

WINE: A crisp, licorice-scented Arneis from Piedmont—perhaps the great 1998 vintage from a superior producer like Giacosa—marches right along with the anise, fennel, and lemon flavors highlighted in this dish.

1. Wash the fennel and cut it, lengthwise, into ⅛-inch-thick pieces. Place the fennel in a shallow baking dish large enough to hold the fish along with the shallots, garlic, and rosemary. Add the oil and pastis and stir to combine. Add the bass and turn it to season well. Cover the entire dish with plastic wrap and place in the refrigerator to marinate for 8 hours or overnight.

2. Preheat and oil the grill.

3. Remove the bass and fennel from the marinade. Using paper towel, pat the bass and fennel dry to prevent flare-ups on the grill. Season both the cavity and outside of the fish with salt and pepper to taste. Place 4 lemon slices into each cavity along with a teaspoon of fennel seeds and 1 bay leaf.

4. Remove the rosemary sprigs from the marinade and set them aside.

5. Place the bass on the preheated grill and grill, turning once, for about 10 minutes or until nicely marked and cooked through. Three minutes before the fish is ready, add the fennel to the grill and cook, turning once, until nicely marked.

6. Place the fennel on a serving platter. Lift the bass from the grill and lay it over the fennel and sprinkle with the basil julienne. Garnish each fish with 1 of the reserved rosemary sprigs. Place mounds of Cured Lemons around the edge of the platter and serve.

NOTE: Anisette is available from fine-quality liquor stores. Pastis or Pernod are good substitutes.

Cooking time will vary depending upon the intensity of the heat of your grill. When the fish is properly grilled, it will peel easily off the bone. You can, if desired, also easily remove the skin and head before serving.

CRAB-CRUSTED SEA BASS WITH BRAISED ENDIVE, PINE NUT POLENTA, AND RED WINE FUMET

SERVES 6

ALTHOUGH THIS IS A RECIPE with many components that might make it complicated for the home cook, it is one of the signature dishes at Tribeca Grill. It evolved when I had to do the fish course for a benefit dinner for eight hundred and needed to come up with a way to cook fish that would keep it moist. The natural oiliness of the bass, the butter in the crust, which serves as a baste, and the final baking all combine to keep the fish at its best. Cooking at home, the crab-crusted bass could be served on its own; however, if you want to make a splash, try to create the whole recipe. Many of the components can be made in advance, so putting the dish together will be a snap at dinnertime just as it is for a chef trying to feed a crowd.

> 1 cup (2 sticks) plus 2 tablespoons unsalted butter, at room temperature
> 3/4 pound lump crabmeat, picked clean of all shell cartilage
> 1/3 cup chopped fresh flat-leaf parsley leaves
> 1/3 cup finely diced red bell pepper
> 1/3 cup finely diced yellow bell pepper
> 1 tablespoon fresh lemon juice
> 2 teaspoons coarse salt, plus more to taste
> 1 teaspoon freshly ground white pepper, plus more to taste
> 1 teaspoon cayenne pepper
> 3/4 cup fresh, white bread crumbs
> Six 6-ounce Chilean sea bass fillets
> 18 steamed asparagus spears
> Pine Nut Polenta (see page 189)
> Braised Endive (see page 190)
> Red Wine Fumet (recipe follows)

1. Place 1 cup of the butter in the bowl of an electric mixer and beat, on high speed, until light and fluffy. Add the crabmeat, parsley, bell peppers, lemon juice, 2 teaspoons salt, 1 teaspoon pepper, and the cayenne and beat to incorporate well. Reduce speed to low and add the bread crumbs. Beat to just combine. Scrape the mixture onto a piece of parchment paper and smooth it out slightly. Place another piece of parchment paper on top and, using a rolling pin, roll the crabmeat mixture out to a ⅛-inch thickness. Lift the parchment to a cookie sheet and place in the refrigerator for at least 1 hour to firm.

2. Preheat the broiler.

3. Pat the fish very dry with a clean kitchen towel. Season it to taste with salt and pepper.

4. Remove the crabmeat crust from the refrigerator and peel off the top layer of parchment. Lay the fish on top of the firm crust and, using a sharp knife, cut around the fish to cut the crust to fit each piece of fish. Flip the fish pieces over and remove the parchment paper. Transfer the fish to a nonstick roasting pan and place under the broiler for 1½ minutes or until the crust is golden brown. Remove from the broiler and reduce the oven temperature to 400°F.

5. Place the fish in the oven and bake for 8 to 10 minutes or until the flesh is cooked through but still moist in the center.

6. While the fish is baking, heat the remaining butter in a large nonstick sauté pan over medium heat. Add the asparagus and salt and pepper to taste and sauté for about 3 minutes or just until the asparagus is heated through.

7. Spoon the polenta into the center of each of six dinner plates. Lay a Braised Endive and 3 spears of asparagus on top of the polenta. Place a piece of the Crab-Crusted Sea Bass on top and spoon some of the Red Wine Fumet around the edge of the plate. Serve immediately.

WINE: For this dish, we recommend a rich, fully flavored Chardonnay from Napa's Markham Vineyards or a soft, supple Pinot Noir from Robert Sinskey in Carneros.

Red Wine Fumet

Makes about 1 cup

1 tablespoon plus 2 teaspoons unsalted butter
1 small shallot, peeled and chopped
¾ cup red wine
½ cup port wine
4 peppercorns
1 bay leaf
1 sprig of fresh thyme
4 cups clam juice
Coarse salt and freshly ground pepper to taste

1. Heat 2 teaspoons of the butter in a medium saucepan over medium heat. Add the shallot and sauté for 3 minutes. Add the red wine and port, peppercorns, bay leaf, and thyme and bring to a boil. Cook, stirring occasionally, for about 10 minutes or until the liquid has reduced by two thirds and is almost syrupy.

2. Raise the heat and add the clam juice. Bring to a boil; lower the heat and simmer for about 30 minutes or until the liquid has reduced to 1 cup. Strain through a fine sieve into a small saucepan. Beat in the remaining tablespoon of butter and season to taste with salt and pepper. If necessary, reheat just before serving.

NOTE: The crab crust may be made up to 1 day in advance. Store, tightly covered and refrigerated.

The Pine Nut Polenta and Braised Endive may be made early in the day and reheated in a low oven. If necessary, beat no more than ¼ cup of heavy cream into the polenta to loosen it if it gets too firm as it sits.

The Red Wine Fumet may be made early in the day without the addition of the last tablespoon of butter. Store, covered and refrigerated. Reheat and beat in the tablespoon of butter just before serving.

SPICE-RUBBED YELLOWFIN TUNA WITH SEAWEED SALAD

SERVES 6

SINCE WE ALWAYS HAVE THE TUNA and sesame noodles on our appetizer menu, I try to come up with other ideas for the ever-popular tuna main course. The spice mixture in this dish seems to be a perfect blend to accentuate the rich, mellow tuna. And the Seaweed Salad brings the right balance and finish to the plate. However, if you have difficulty finding the goma wakame, feel free to use any salad greens that you might have on hand.

¼ cup cracked black pepper
¼ cup toasted coriander seeds, ground
1½ tablespoons chopped flat-leaf parsley leaves
1 tablespoon chopped fresh cilantro leaves
1 tablespoon chopped fresh thyme leaves
Six 6-ounce, 1-inch-thick tuna loin steaks
Coarse salt to taste
2 tablespoons canola oil
1 cup goma wakame (seasoned seaweed salad) (see Note)
1 cup julienned hothouse (seedless) cucumber
½ cup enoki mushrooms
⅓ cup julienned daikon radish
⅓ cup julienned carrot
⅓ cup radish sprouts
1 cup Lemon-Caper Vinaigrette (see page 231)
Freshly ground pepper to taste
1 cup warm Beurre Blanc (see page 234)

> **WINE:** A meaty, earthy Burgundy like a Pommard Clos des Epenots from Comte Armand has the body and spiciness to complement the tuna and the depth of flavor to pair with the seaweed and coriander.

Pan-Seared Snapper with Toasted Couscous

Serves 6

THE MARINIÈRE IN THIS RECIPE comes from Georges Blanc, one of the world's greatest chefs. His signature dish, Bar à la Marinière, was its inspiration. This simple sauce with wonderfully harmonious flavors goes incredibly well with any fin fish. On the other hand, the couscous is a typical Israeli peasant dish that, in recent years, has found a comfortable spot on American restaurant tables (much to the amusement of visiting Israelis).

3 tablespoons unsalted butter
1 cup diced onion
2 cups Israeli couscous (see Note)
4 cups hot Chicken Stock (see page 229) or canned chicken broth
1 teaspoon saffron threads
Coarse salt and freshly ground pepper to taste
¼ cup finely diced leek, white and light-green part only, blanched
¼ cup finely diced tomato
3 tablespoons olive oil
2 teaspoons minced garlic
1½ pounds fresh spinach, stems removed, blanched
1 cup Beurre Blanc (see page 234)
2 tablespoons Marinière (see page 234)
2 teaspoons fresh lemon juice
1 teaspoon soy sauce
1 tablespoon chopped flat-leaf parsley leaves
2 tablespoons vegetable oil
Six 6-ounce red snapper fillets, skin on
¼ cup chopped fresh chives

WINE: To partner with the substance and texture of this dish, a full-bodied white Rhone wine with texture and complexity of its own, such as Beaucastel's Roussanne Vieilles Vignes, is required.

1. Heat the butter in a medium saucepan over medium heat. Add the onion and sauté for 4 minutes or until just soft. Stir in the couscous and sauté for about 2 minutes or until the couscous is slightly toasted. Add the hot stock or broth and the saffron and bring to a boil. Season to taste with salt and pepper. Cover and simmer for about 10 minutes or until the liquid has been absorbed. Remove from the heat and stir in the leek and the tomato. Taste and, if necessary, adjust the seasoning with salt and pepper. Cover and keep warm until ready to serve.

2. Heat the olive oil in a large sauté pan over medium heat. Add the garlic and sauté for 3 minutes or until the garlic begins to color. Immediately add the spinach and sauté for about 3 minutes or just until the spinach is wilted. Remove from the heat and season to taste with salt and pepper. Tent lightly with aluminum foil to keep warm.

 THE TRIBECA GRILL COOKBOOK

3. Place the Beurre Blanc in a small saucepan over medium heat and bring to a gentle simmer. Whisk in the Marinière until well combined. Add the lemon juice and soy sauce and whisk to blend. Add the parsley and season to taste with salt and pepper. Tent lightly with aluminum foil to keep warm.

4. Heat the vegetable oil in a large sauté pan over medium heat. Season the snapper with salt and pepper to taste. When the oil is very hot but not smoking, place the snapper in the pan, skin side down, pressing lightly with a spatula to flatten the fish as it cooks. Sear for 3 minutes; turn and sear the remaining side for 3 minutes or until the fish is just cooked through. Using a spatula, remove the fish from the pan and drain on a double layer of paper towel.

5. Place a 4-inch ring mold in the center of each of six dinner plates (if you only have one ring mold, working quickly, do one plate at a time). Spoon equal portions of spinach into each mold. Top with equal portions of couscous, pressing down to compact the mold. Carefully lift off the ring mold. Place a snapper fillet on top of the couscous. Drizzle the warm butter sauce over the snapper and around the edge of the plate. Sprinkle with chopped chives and serve.

NOTE: Israeli couscous, a large-grained starch quite different from the more-familiar North African fine-grained semolina, is available from Middle Eastern markets and specialty food stores.

PAELLA QUISBERT

JULIO QUISBERT, OUR FORMER BANQUET CHEF, is responsible for this incredibly good paella. While it began as a Friday special, it quickly moved to parties and banquets, where it has starred. It is easy to make and simply delicious. Try it for entertaining at home with a big salad, some garlic bread, and lots and lots of great wine.

3 cups water
1 teaspoon saffron threads
2 cups long-grain rice
Coarse salt and freshly ground pepper to taste
6 tablespoons olive oil
1 red bell pepper, cored, seeded, and diced
1 yellow bell pepper, cored, seeded, and diced
1½ cups finely diced onions
2 teaspoons minced garlic
1 cup dry white wine
2 cups bottled clam juice
24 mussels
24 Manila or other small clams
½ pound medium shrimp, peeled and deveined
½ pound bay scallops
½ pound calamari, cleaned and cut into rings
½ cup fresh green peas, blanched
½ cup chopped fresh flat-leaf parsley leaves

WINE: A floral-scented, aromatic, and crisp Albariño from the Rias Baixas region is a good match for the seafood mix and the saffron.

1. Place the water in a large saucepan over medium heat. Add the saffron and allow it to "bloom." Add the rice and salt and pepper to taste. Cover and cook for about 20 minutes or until the rice is al dente.

2. Heat 2 tablespoons of the olive oil in a large sauté pan over medium heat. Add the bell peppers and 1 cup of the onions and sauté for about 5 minutes or until just softened. Remove from the heat.

3. Heat 1 tablespoon of the olive oil in a saucepan over medium heat. Add ½ teaspoon of the garlic and the remaining onion and sauté for 3 minutes. Add the wine and bring to a boil. Lower the heat and simmer for about 8 minutes or until the wine is reduced by one half. Add the clam juice and simmer for 10 minutes. Add the mussels and clams and cover. Cook for about 4 minutes or until the shells have opened and the meat is cooked. Remove from the heat.

4. Heat 1 tablespoon of olive oil and ½ teaspoon of garlic in a large sauté pan over medium heat. Add the shrimp and salt and pepper to taste and sauté for about 2 minutes or until the shrimp is pink. Using a slotted spoon, lift the shrimp from the pan and set aside.

5. Wipe the pan clean and return it to medium heat. Add another tablespoon of oil and ½ teaspoon of garlic to the pan. Add the scallops and salt and pepper to taste and sauté for 1 minute or until the scallops are just opaque. Using a slotted spoon, lift the scallops from the pan and set aside.

6. Wipe the pan clean and return it to medium heat. Add the remaining 1 tablespoon of olive oil and ½ teaspoon of garlic to the pan. Add the calamari and sauté for 1 minute or until the calamari is opaque. Using a slotted spoon, lift the calamari from the pan and set aside.

7. Add the pepper-onion mixture, the mussel-clam mixture, the shrimp, scallops, calamari, peas, and parsley to the rice, tossing to combine. Return to low heat and cook for about 5 minutes or until the paella is hot.

8. Scoop the paella into large, shallow soup or pasta bowls and serve.

NOTE: You can, if desired, add grilled chicken or chorizo sausage to the paella in addition to or in place of some of the seafood.

Spicy Mussels with Baby Bok Choy

Serves 6

When I was hired by Drew Nieporent and Robert De Niro to head up the kitchen at their new restaurant, I was on the eve of fulfilling my travel fantasy of visiting Southeast Asia. Although I was expected back in eight weeks, I ended up in Asia for seven months before the restaurant was ready for my return. One of the first recipes that I developed for the newly opened Tribeca Grill was this one. Based on a recipe for iguana that I had eaten in a small village outside Chiang-Mai, Thailand, its spicy, heady broth intensifies the sweetness of the mussels. In 1990, ingredients that I had tasted in Asia such as the Kaffir lime leaves, lemongrass, and baby bok choy (all used in the recipe) had not yet made their way into mainstream American cooking. Nor had iguana, but I doubt that it ever will.

1 medium red bell pepper
1 medium yellow bell pepper
4 heads baby bok choy
½ teaspoon coarse salt, plus more to taste
Freshly ground pepper to taste
2 tablespoons olive oil
One 2-inch piece fresh ginger, minced
4 cloves garlic, minced
3 shallots, peeled and minced
2 Kaffir lime leaves, sliced (see Note, page 125)
2 stalks lemongrass, well trimmed and finely chopped (see Note)
2 tablespoons Thai red curry paste (see Note)
6 cups clam juice
2 cups unsweetened coconut milk

WINE: The spice in this dish needs a fruity, concentrated Gewürztraminer such as a Martinelli or Navarro from California.

3 pounds (about 6 dozen) mussels, well cleaned (see Note)
3 cups dry white wine
¼ cup chopped scallions
¼ cup chopped fresh basil leaves
2 tablespoons chopped fresh mint leaves

1. Core and seed the red and yellow bell peppers. Cut each one into ¼-inch dice and set aside.

2. Place about 12 ice cubes in a bowl of very cold water. Set aside.

3. Trim any damaged leaves from the bok choy. Cut each piece in half, length-wise. Bring 2 cups of water to a boil in a medium saucepan over high heat. Add the bok choy and blanch for 2 minutes. Using a slotted spoon, remove the bok choy from the boiling water and immerse it in the reserved ice water bath to prevent further cooking. When cool, drain well and pat dry. Season to taste with salt and pepper and set aside.

4. Heat the oil in a large sauté pan over medium heat. Add the ginger, garlic, shallots, Kaffir lime leaves, lemongrass, and curry paste. Cook, stirring frequently, for 3 minutes or until the vegetables are soft and the aroma very fragrant. Raise the heat and add the clam juice. Bring to a boil. Immediately lower the

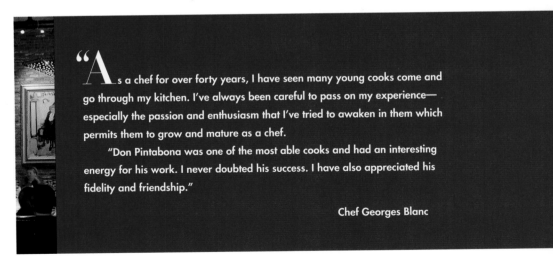

"As a chef for over forty years, I have seen many young cooks come and go through my kitchen. I've always been careful to pass on my experience—especially the passion and enthusiasm that I've tried to awaken in them which permits them to grow and mature as a chef.

"Don Pintabona was one of the most able cooks and had an interesting energy for his work. I never doubted his success. I have also appreciated his fidelity and friendship."

Chef Georges Blanc

heat and simmer for 10 minutes or until the mixture has reduced by one half. Stir in the coconut milk. Return to a simmer and allow to cook, stirring occasionally, for about 10 minutes or until the mixture has thickened slightly. Remove from the heat. Cover lightly and keep warm.

5. Combine the mussels with the wine in a large saucepan over high heat. Bring to a boil. Cover and cook for about 3 minutes or until the shells open. Add the reserved coconut sauce and bell peppers along with the scallions and basil and simmer for an additional 2 minutes. Taste and adjust the seasoning with salt and pepper.

6. Remove and discard any mussels that have not opened. Ladle the mussels with their sauce into six shallow soup bowls. Place a bok choy half on opposite sides of each bowl. Garnish the top with mint and serve immediately.

NOTE: Lemongrass can be rather woody. Be sure that you trim it well and use only the most tender part of the stalk. If you can't find lemongrass, ½ teaspoon freshly grated lime zest makes an excellent substitute for 1 stalk.

Thai red curry paste is available at Asian markets and many specialty food stores.

To clean mussels: Soak mussels in cold water for 10 minutes to allow some of the sand to leach out. Scrub the surface of each shell and, using your fingers, pull away the beard (the dark, shaggy material that protrudes from the end of each mussel). You might have to use a little force. If you don't readily notice the beard, it simply means that it has been removed previously by the seller. Discard any mussels that do not open after being cooked, as they are often inedible.

You can, if desired, serve the mussels over Coconut Rice (see page 187).

THE TRIBECA GRILL COOKBOOK

Poultry, Meat,

and Game

HERB-ROASTED CHICKEN WITH PORCINI GRAVY

CILANTRO- AND SAKE-GRILLED CHICKEN WITH SPICY THAI DRESSING

STUFFED CORNISH GAME HEN WITH PINE NUTS AND RAISINS

HONEY-GLAZED SQUAB WITH WARM LENTILS AND LEMON-OLIVE SAUCE

BARBECUED BREAST OF DUCK WITH PEANUT-WHIPPED POTATOES

GRILLED RIB-EYE OF BEEF WITH WARM POTATOES, BACON, AND LEEKS

HERB-CRUSTED RACK OF LAMB WITH YUKON SCALLION POTATOES

GRILLED DOUBLE-THICK VEAL CHOP WITH GARLIC-HERB BUTTER AND
PROVENÇAL VEGETABLE TART

MOLASSES-CURED PORK LOIN WITH BOSTON BAKED BEANS

MUSHROOM-CRUSTED LOIN OF VENISON WITH BLACK PEPPER SPAETZLE

Herb-Roasted Chicken with Porcini Gravy

SERVES 6

THIS IS THE TRIBECA GRILL's old-fashioned Blue Plate Special, which is always served with Whipped Potatoes (see page 183). We make the standard home-style indentation in the center of the potatoes and fill it with gravy overflowing onto the plate. The only difference from the diner variety is the rich, meaty flavor of the porcini mushrooms in the gravy.

2 ounces (about ½ cup) dried porcini
2 cups hot Chicken Stock (see page 229) or canned chicken broth
Two 3½-pound roasting chickens, preferably free-range and organic
2 tablespoons minced fresh thyme leaves
2 tablespoons minced fresh tarragon leaves
2 tablespoons minced fresh sage leaves
1 tablespoon minced garlic
2 medium onions, peeled
20 whole cloves
1 orange, well washed and halved, crosswise
1 lemon, well washed and halved, crosswise
½ cup (1 stick) unsalted butter, at room temperature
Coarse salt and freshly ground pepper to taste
1 shallot, peeled and minced
5 black peppercorns
2 allspice berries
½ cup dry white wine
1 tablespoon all-purpose flour
2 tablespoons sour cream

WINE: Au Bon Climat or Sanford from the Santa Barbara region of California produces an excellent, ripe, medium-bodied Pinot Noir that would drink well with the chicken and the earthy mushroom gravy.

1. Place the porcini in the hot Chicken Stock or broth to rehydrate for at least 1 hour.

2. Remove the gizzards and livers from the chickens and chop them into fine pieces. Set aside and reserve for the gravy.

3. Fill a large mixing bowl with lightly salted cold water and, one at a time, rinse each chicken well in the salted water. Place the rinsed chickens under cold running water to remove excess salt. Drain well and pat dry.

4. Preheat the oven to 450°F.

5. Combine half of the thyme, tarragon, and sage with the garlic. Using your fingertips, gently pull the skin away from the chicken breast and place the herb-garlic mixture onto the breast meat, taking care not to tear the skin or to create a pocket that is too loose.

6. Stud each onion with an equal number of cloves. Place 1 onion and one half of the orange and lemon into the cavity of each chicken. Using all but 1 tablespoon of the butter, generously coat each chicken with a nice layer of softened butter and season to taste with salt and pepper.

7. Place the chickens on a rack in a large roasting pan with enough water to come up about 1 inch from the bottom of the pan but without touching the rack. Cover the entire pan with aluminum foil and place into the preheated oven. Immediately turn the heat down to 350°F and roast for 30 minutes. Remove the foil and stir in the remaining herbs. Continue roasting, basting every 10 minutes with the pan drippings, for about 45 minutes to 1 hour or until the skin is golden and an instant-read thermometer inserted into the thickest part of the chicken reads 155°F.

8. While the chicken is roasting, prepare the gravy.

9. Using a slotted spoon, lift the rehydrated porcini from the stock (or broth), separately reserving the stock. Roughly chop the porcini and set them aside.

10. Heat the remaining 1 tablespoon of butter in a medium sauté pan over medium heat. Add the shallot, peppercorns, and allspice, along with the reserved gizzards and livers, and sauté for about 3 minutes or until the meat

begins to take on some color. Add the wine and cook, stirring occasionally, for about 5 minutes or until the pan is almost dry.

11. Whisk the flour into the sauté pan, whisking until a smooth mixture forms. Spoon ¼ cup of pan drippings (including the fat) from the chicken and whisk it into the flour. Add the reserved mushroom soaking liquid and salt and pepper to taste and bring to a simmer. Lower the heat and simmer, stirring frequently, for about 15 minutes or until the flour has absorbed the flavors and the gravy has thickened.

12. Strain the gravy through a fine sieve into a clean saucepan. Place the saucepan over low heat and whisk in the sour cream and reserved porcini. Taste and, if necessary, season with salt and pepper.

13. Remove the chickens from the oven and carve into serving pieces. Serve with the Porcini Gravy and, if desired, Whipped Potatoes.

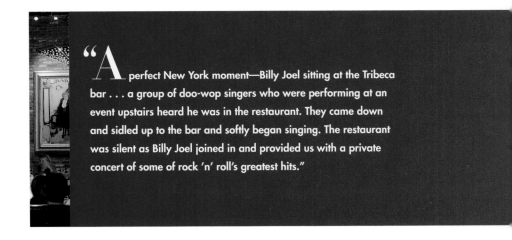

"A perfect New York moment—Billy Joel sitting at the Tribeca bar . . . a group of doo-wop singers who were performing at an event upstairs heard he was in the restaurant. They came down and sidled up to the bar and softly began singing. The restaurant was silent as Billy Joel joined in and provided us with a private concert of some of rock 'n' roll's greatest hits."

Cilantro- and Sake-Grilled Chicken with Spicy Thai Dressing

SERVES 6

THE ASIAN FLAVORS OF BOTH THE MARINADE and the sauce make this an especially tasty but very low-fat dish. Although perfect for the summertime grill, the chicken also grills nicely in a stovetop grill pan. Don't be intimidated by the length of the recipe—it's got quite a few ingredients, but it is very simple to prepare.

8 cloves garlic
¾ cup plus 2 tablespoons olive oil
1 medium onion, sliced
1-inch piece fresh ginger, peeled and chopped
2 cups water
1 cup sake (see Note, page 48)
1½ cups chopped fresh cilantro leaves
½ cup soy sauce
¼ cup rice wine vinegar (see Note, page 48)
2 star anise
1 tablespoon curry powder
1 teaspoon turmeric
6 French-style (skin on, bone in, wing intact) chicken breast halves or 6 skinless, boneless chicken breast halves
1 cup diced onion
1 cup fresh cilantro leaves
3 whole scallions, chopped
1 stalk lemongrass, chopped (see page 148)

WINE: A full-bodied white with a nice note of spice such as Central Coast's Treana Blanc, a mixture of Viognier and Marsanne, more than meets the flavors of this dish.

THE TRIBECA GRILL COOKBOOK

2 medium red bell peppers, cored, seeded, and diced
¼ cup red wine vinegar
3 tablespoons nam pla (Thai fish sauce) (see Note, page 51)
1 tablespoon sriracha (smooth Thai chili paste) (see Note, page 51)
Coarse salt and freshly ground pepper to taste
1 tablespoon cornstarch dissolved in 1 tablespoon cold water, optional

1. Finely chop 5 cloves of garlic and separately slice the remaining 3 cloves. Set aside.

2. Heat ¼ cup of the olive oil in a medium sauté pan over medium-low heat. Add the chopped garlic, sliced onion, and ginger and cook, stirring frequently, for about 5 minutes or until the vegetables have softened but not browned.

3. Scrape the vegetables into a bowl. Stir in 1 cup of water and ½ cup of the sake along with the chopped cilantro, soy sauce, rice wine vinegar, star anise, curry powder, and turmeric.

4. Place the chicken in a nonreactive baking dish. Pour the marinade over the chicken and cover with plastic wrap. Refrigerate and allow to marinate for no less than 1 hour or up to 5 hours, turning the chicken from time to time.

5. While the chicken is marinating, prepare the dressing. Heat 2 tablespoons of the remaining olive oil in a medium saucepan over medium-low heat. Add the reserved sliced garlic along with the diced onion and cook, stirring frequently, for 3 minutes. Do not brown.

6. Stir in the cilantro leaves, scallions, and lemongrass. Cook, stirring frequently, for an additional 3 minutes.

7. Add the remaining 1 cup of water, ½ cup of sake, and ½ cup of olive oil along with the diced bell peppers, red wine vinegar, nam pla, and sriracha. Raise the heat and bring to a boil. Immediately reduce the heat and allow the dressing to just barely simmer for 15 minutes.

8. Pour the dressing into a blender and process until very smooth. Taste and adjust the seasoning with salt and pepper, if necessary.

9. Pour the dressing through a fine sieve into a clean saucepan and cover lightly.

10. Preheat and oil the grill.

11. Remove the chicken from the marinade and place it, skin side down, on the hot grill. Grill, turning frequently, for about 15 minutes or until the chicken is cooked through. (If the grill is extremely hot and the skin begins to blacken before the chicken is thoroughly cooked, remove the chicken from the grill and finish cooking it—to 155 F on an instant-read thermometer—in a preheated 350 F oven. You will still have the taste of the grill without the unpleasant-tasting burned skin.)

12. While the chicken is grilling, reheat the dressing over medium heat. If you find that it is too thin, thicken it slightly with a slurry made from 1 tablespoon of cornstarch dissolved in 1 tablespoon cold water. Pour half of the slurry into the dressing, whisking constantly as you pour. Cook, whisking constantly, for 2 minutes or until the dressing begins to thicken. If it is still too thin, add the remaining slurry as above.

13. Serve the chicken with the warm dressing spooned over the top. Suggested side dishes might be some Coconut Rice (see page 187), jasmine or basmati rice, and a simple steamed vegetable.

STUFFED CORNISH GAME HEN WITH PINE NUTS AND RAISINS

SERVES 6

THIS IS AN ELEGANT YET EASY-TO-PREPARE dish for at-home entertaining. Although large hens are meaty enough to serve two people, I usually like to serve smaller birds, allowing one whole bird per person. The pine nuts and raisins lend typically Sicilian flavors to the stuffing and take the dish a little out of the ordinary. Almost any steamed or roasted vegetable will pair well with the roasted hens.

½ cup raisins
¼ cup apple brandy or cognac
1 loaf stale sliced white bread
6 small Cornish game hens
2 tablespoons olive oil
6 tablespoons unsalted butter, at room temperature
1 cup finely diced celery
½ cup finely diced onion
2 tablespoons minced garlic
½ cup chopped flat-leaf parsley leaves
½ cup toasted pine nuts
*Approximately 1½ cups Chicken Stock (see page 229)
   or canned chicken broth*
Coarse salt and freshly ground pepper to taste
1 teaspoon paprika

> **WINE:** A tropical, fruit-flavored California Chardonnay such as ZD is a great match for the sweetness of the stuffing and the rich, meaty hen.

1. Preheat the oven to 350°F.

2. Combine the raisins and brandy in a small bowl. Set aside for about 15 minutes to allow the raisins to plump slightly.

3. Trim the crusts from the bread and cut the slices into ½-inch cubes. Place the bread cubes on a baking sheet in the preheated oven and bake for about 15 minutes or until golden brown. Remove from the oven and transfer the cubes to a mixing bowl. Set aside. Do not turn off the oven.

4. Fill a large mixing bowl with lightly salted cold water and, one at a time, thoroughly rinse each hen in the salted water. Place the rinsed hens under cold running water to remove excess salt. Drain well and pat dry. Set aside.

5. Drain the liquid from the raisins, separately reserving both the raisins and the liquid.

6. Combine the oil with 2 tablespoons of the butter in a medium sauté pan over medium heat. Add the celery, onion, and 1 tablespoon of the garlic and sauté for 3 minutes. Add the reserved soaking liquid from the raisins and cook, stirring frequently, for about 5 minutes or until the liquid has evaporated. Stir in the parsley, pine nuts, and reserved raisins. Scrape the mixture into the reserved toasted bread cubes and add just enough Chicken Stock or broth to moisten without letting the bread cubes get soggy. Season to taste with salt and pepper.

7. Using a large spoon, lightly push some stuffing into the cavity of each bird. (Do not pack the stuffing in tightly or it will get very soggy and may not cook properly.)

8. Combine the remaining butter and garlic and coat each hen with a light layer of the seasoned butter. Sprinkle lightly with paprika and season to taste with salt and pepper.

9. Place the hens in a roasting pan. Cover the pan with aluminum foil and place in the preheated oven. Roast for 20 minutes. Remove the foil and continue to roast for an additional 20 minutes or until the hens are golden brown and an instant-read thermometer inserted into the center of the bird and into the stuffing reads 165°F. Remove from the oven and serve.

Barbecued Breast of Duck with Peanut-Whipped Potatoes

Serves 6

ONE OF THE MEATS THAT I FIND most compatible with the Asian ingredients that I am partial to is duck. I almost always have some type of duck on the menu, quite frequently breast of duck, which is lean and richly flavored. In this recipe, the barbecue glaze beautifully caramelizes the duck and the Peanut-Whipped Potatoes make a welcome nest for the juices. For an extra Asian treat on the plate, garnish it with Pickled Japanese Eggplant (see page 237) and some sautéed baby bok choy.

4 teaspoons peanut oil
2 shallots, peeled and chopped
½ tablespoon Thai red curry paste (see Note, page 148)
¾ cup hoisin sauce (see Note)
2 cups Chicken Stock (see page 229) or canned chicken broth
½ cup soy sauce
1 teaspoon honey
8 cloves garlic, peeled
1 stalk lemongrass, minced (see page 148)
1-inch piece fresh ginger, peeled and minced
2 tablespoons minced fresh cilantro leaves
1 tablespoon five spice powder (see Note)
6 Long Island duck breast halves, skin on, trimmed
  of excess fat, with wing bone attached and cleaned
  (see Note)
1 tablespoon vegetable oil
Coarse salt and freshly ground pepper to taste
Peanut-Whipped Potatoes (see Note on page 183)

WINE: The complexity of this dish stands up well to a high-alcohol, concentrated, spicy Zinfandel, such as a single vineyard Turley or Martinelli's Jackass Hill.

1. Heat the oil in a medium saucepan over medium heat. Add the shallots and curry paste and sauté for 3 minutes. Stir in the hoisin, Chicken Stock or broth, soy sauce, honey, garlic, lemongrass, ginger, cilantro, and five spice powder and bring to a boil. Immediately lower the heat and simmer for 2 minutes. Remove from the heat and allow to cool.

2. Place the duck breasts in a shallow baking pan and pour the cooled sauce over them, turning to coat nicely. Cover with plastic wrap and set aside to marinate for 1 hour.

3. Cover the grill rack with aluminum foil (the foil will keep the fatty duck from causing flare-ups and burning over the hot flame). Preheat the grill. Using a pastry brush, lightly coat the foil with vegetable oil.

4. Remove the duck from the marinade and pat off excess sauce (to prevent grill flare-ups). Season to taste with salt and pepper. Place the breasts, skin side down, on the hot grill and cook for 3 minutes. Turn and grill the remaining side for 3 minutes. Continue to grill the duck, turning every 30 seconds to prevent burning, for an additional 3 minutes for medium. (If you wish well-done duck—which I personally don't recommend—you will have to finish the cooking in a preheated 400°F oven to avoid blackening the skin.) Remove the duck from the grill and place it on a platter to rest for about 3 minutes before slicing.

5. Spoon equal portions of the Peanut-Whipped Potatoes into the center of each of six dinner plates. Slice each duck breast, on the bias, into 5 slices. Keeping the sliced breasts together, place 1 breast on the potatoes in each plate, slightly fanning the slices out over the potatoes. If desired, you can serve Pickled Japanese Eggplant or sautéed Chinese broccoli or baby bok choy on the side.

NOTE: Hoisin sauce and five spice powder are available from Asian markets and specialty food stores.

You might want to buy 3 whole ducks and break them down yourself, reserving the legs for Duck Confit (see page 239) and the bodies for stock. Duck breasts with the wing attached are available from D'Artagnan (see Sources).

CLOCKWISE FROM UPPER RIGHT:
Mushroom-Crusted Loin of Venison with Black Pepper Spaetzle,
Barbecued Breast of Duck with Peanut-Whipped Potatoes,
Herb-Roasted Chicken with Porcini Gravy

GRILLED RIB-EYE OF BEEF WITH WARM POTATOES, BACON, AND LEEKS

SERVES 6

THIS IS ABOUT AS STRAIGHTFORWARD A RECIPE as you can get. The smokiness of the bacon melds well with the grilled flavor of the steak to create a very homey taste. It is a simple combination of flavors that seems to say "picnic" or outdoor dining. In fact, the potatoes, on their own, make a great side dish for a barbecue, picnic, or deck dining. The Natural Jus adds a restaurant touch, but if you don't have time to make it, just serve up some good old-fashioned steak and potatoes.

6 ounces slab bacon, finely diced
1 cup diced leeks, white part only
½ cup finely diced shallots
¾ cup olive oil
¼ cup sherry wine vinegar
1 tablespoon Dijon mustard
2 pounds Yukon gold potatoes
Coarse salt and freshly ground pepper to taste
¼ cup chopped flat-leaf parsley leaves
Six 1-inch-thick rib-eye steaks, trimmed of excess fat
Natural Jus, optional (see page 235)

> **WINE:** To provide the smokiness and body required to stand up to the bacon and rich beef, a Côte-Rôtie from Guigal or Rostang will make the perfect drinking statement.

1. Place the bacon in a large sauté pan over medium-low heat. Cook, stirring frequently, for about 10 minutes or until the fat is rendered out and the bacon bits are very crisp. If necessary, lower the heat to keep the bacon from burning.

2. Add the leeks and shallots and sauté for 3 minutes or just until the vegetables are soft. Remove from the heat.

3. Whisk together the oil, vinegar, and mustard.

4. Place the potatoes in a large saucepan, with cold, salted water to cover by 1 inch, over high heat. Bring to a boil; lower the heat and simmer for 20 minutes or until the potatoes are tender when pierced with the point of a small, sharp knife. Remove from the heat and drain well. Working quickly, push the peels off the potatoes and cut the potatoes into large chunks. Immediately, place the warm potatoes in a mixing bowl and add the warm bacon mixture, tossing to combine (see Note). Pour the mustard mixture over the top and season to taste with salt and pepper. Toss to combine. Sprinkle the top with the parsley. Cover lightly and keep warm.

5. Preheat and oil the grill.

6. Season the steaks with salt and pepper to taste. Place them on the hot grill and cook, turning once, for 8 to 10 minutes for medium-rare.

7. Spoon equal portions of the warm potato mixture onto each of six plates. Place a steak on top and, if desired, drizzle the plate with Natural Jus and serve.

NOTE: The warmer the potatoes, the more of the vinaigrette they will absorb, so you must work quickly and carefully while they are still hot.

Herb-Crusted Rack of Lamb with Yukon Scallion Potatoes

SERVES 6

RACK OF LAMB IS PROBABLY the most popular meat on both the restaurant and banquet menu. We have endless variations on the theme but, without a doubt, this recipe is the most requested by customers and staff alike. Almost any potato would be a nice accompaniment—even a simple roasted potato—but Yukon-Scallion Potatoes are an especially delicious addition to the plate.

1 cup blended olive oil
1 shallot, peeled and chopped
1 clove garlic, peeled and chopped
1 tablespoon minced fresh rosemary leaves
1 tablespoon minced fresh thyme leaves
1 tablespoon coarsely ground black pepper
3 baby racks of lamb, bones cleaned and Frenched (see Note)
1 cup fresh Italian-seasoned bread crumbs
1 teaspoon dried basil
1 teaspoon dried thyme
1 teaspoon dried oregano
1 teaspoon dried rosemary
Coarse salt and freshly ground pepper to taste
Natural Jus, optional (see page 235)
1 cup grainy mustard
2 tablespoons peanut oil
Yukon Scallion Potatoes (see page 186)
6 sprigs of fresh rosemary
½ cup Mint Oil, optional (see page 236)

> **WINE:** This is a classic—Cabernet Sauvignon and lamb! A California Cabernet like Caymus or a Bordeaux like Château Cos D'Estournel are just two of many that make the perfect match.

1. Combine the blended oil, shallot, garlic, rosemary, thyme, and pepper in a shallow glass baking dish. Add the lamb and turn to coat all sides. Cover with plastic wrap and refrigerate, turning occasionally, for 8 hours (or overnight).

2. Combine the bread crumbs with the dried basil, thyme, oregano, and rosemary. Stir in the salt and pepper to taste and set aside.

3. Preheat the oven to 450°F.

4. If using, place the Natural Jus in a small saucepan over low heat and bring to a simmer. Remove from the heat and cover lightly to keep warm.

5. Remove the lamb from the marinade and pat it dry. Using a pastry brush, generously coat the lamb with the grainy mustard. Roll the mustard-coated lamb in the bread crumb mixture.

6. Heat the peanut oil in a large sauté pan over medium-high heat. Add the racks and sear each side for about 2 minutes or until nicely browned. Transfer the racks to a roasting pan. Place in the preheated oven and roast for about 20 minutes or until the racks are well browned and an instant-read thermometer inserted into the thickest part reads 145°F for rare or 155°F for medium. Remove from the oven and allow to rest for about 3 minutes before carving.

7. Place a scoop of Yukon Scallion Potatoes in the center of each of six plates. Cut each rack into 8 chops and place 4 chops on the potatoes on each plate. If using, drizzle Natural Jus over the lamb and around the edge of the plate. Garnish with a sprig of rosemary and serve.

NOTE: Frenched baby rack of lamb is available from quality butchers, some specialty food stores, or by mail order from D'Artagnan (see Sources).

GRILLED DOUBLE-THICK VEAL CHOP WITH GARLIC-HERB BUTTER AND PROVENÇAL VEGETABLE TART

SERVES 6

THE GARLIC-BUTTER STUFFING in this veal chop makes a wonderful sauce for the delicate veal. Although you don't need the tart to enjoy the veal, it certainly makes a beautiful presentation, plus the flavors marry so well with the meat. Like many restaurant preparations, the tart takes some time to create, but is quick on the "pickup," which also helps the home cook.

Six 1½-inch-thick veal loin chops
¾ cup (1½ sticks) unsalted butter, at room temperature
2 tablespoons freshly grated lemon zest
2 tablespoons minced fresh rosemary needles
1 tablespoon minced fresh chives
1 tablespoon minced fresh thyme leaves
1 tablespoon minced fresh parsley leaves
8 ripe plum tomatoes, well washed and cored
2 Japanese eggplants, well washed and trimmed
1 large zucchini, well washed and trimmed
1 large yellow squash, well washed and trimmed
¼ cup olive oil
2 tablespoons fresh lemon juice
Coarse salt and freshly ground pepper to taste
3 tablespoons melted unsalted butter
½ cup fresh bread crumbs
6 fresh herb sprigs (rosemary, parsley, or thyme)

WINE: A red Burgundy such as a Beaune Cent Vignes from Albert Morot in a superior year like 1996 has the grip, structure, and ripeness to match the expansiveness of this dish.

1. With a very sharp knife, make a 2-inch-long incision along the outside center and into the core of the veal chop to create a deep pocket.

2. Combine the room-temperature butter with the lemon zest and minced rosemary, chives, thyme, and parsley. When well blended, scrape the butter mixture into a pastry bag fitted with a ½-inch tip. Pipe about 2 tablespoons of the butter into the pocket of each veal chop. Using a toothpick, close the pocket. Transfer the chops to a platter and cover lightly with plastic wrap. Place in the refrigerator for 1 hour.

3. Using a chef's knife, Japanese vegetable slicer or a mandoline (see page 19), cut the plum tomatoes, eggplants, zucchini, and yellow squash into thin slices (*top photo*). Place the vegetable slices in a mixing bowl and add the olive oil and lemon juice, along with salt and pepper to taste, tossing to coat well.

4. Using a pastry brush, lightly coat a nonstick baking sheet small enough to fit under the broiler with some of the melted butter. Set aside.

5. Preheat the broiler.

6. Starting with zucchini, make a 3-inch round circle of slightly overlapping vegetable slices, filling in until a complete circle of zucchini has been made (*second photo*). Season the zucchini with salt and pepper to taste. Continue making layers and seasoning each one, following the zucchini with alternating slices of yellow squash and eggplant, followed by yellow squash and a final circle of tomato. Continue making tarts until you have prepared 6. Sprinkle the tops with bread crumbs (*third photo*).

7. Using a spatula, carefully transfer the tarts to the prepared baking sheet. Using a pastry brush, lightly coat the tops of the tarts with melted butter. Season to taste with salt and pepper and place under the broiler for 3 minutes or until the tops begin to brown. Remove from the broiler and set aside (*bottom photo*). Set the oven temperature to 350°F.

8. Preheat and oil the grill. Alternately, preheat a stovetop grill or the broiler.

9. Remove the veal chops from the refrigerator and season to taste with salt and pepper.

10. Place the chops on the hot grill (or on the stovetop grill or under the broiler) and grill for 3 minutes. Rotate the chops about 90 degrees and grill for an additional 2 minutes to create crosshatch grill marks. Turn and grill for 3 minutes; again, rotate the chops about 90 degrees and grill for an additional 2 minutes to create crosshatch grill marks. Remove from the grill.

11. While the meat is grilling, place the tarts in the preheated oven and bake for about 8 minutes or until the vegetables are almost cooked through and the tops are golden.

12. Place a vegetable tart at the top of each of six plates. Place a veal chop below each tart. Remove the toothpick from the veal, allowing the butter sauce to leak onto the plate. Garnish with a fresh herb sprig and serve.

MOLASSES-CURED PORK LOIN WITH BOSTON BAKED BEANS

SERVES 6

WHENEVER I DO FOOD PROMOTIONS—especially in Asia—I try to do dishes that are, without question, very American. Often I return to those dishes that are similar to the ones I learned working with Charlie Palmer at the River Café and Aureole. This particular "all-American" recipe was prepared at the Four Seasons in Singapore and then made its way to the Tribeca menu.

4 cups warm water
1 cup unsulfured molasses
¼ cup Southern Comfort liqueur
¼ cup pure maple syrup
1 tablespoon pure vanilla extract
1 cinnamon stick
1 whole clove
1 bay leaf
½ teaspoon allspice berries
One 4-pound boneless pork loin, trimmed of excess fat
Coarse salt and freshly ground pepper to taste

WINE: A jammy, berry-flavored Shiraz from Australia would perfectly partner the sweetness of this complex dish.

1. Combine the water, molasses, liqueur, maple syrup, vanilla, cinnamon stick, clove, bay leaf, and allspice berries in a mixing bowl, stirring until well blended.

2. Place the pork loin in a shallow baking dish (preferably glass) and pour the molasses mixture over the pork, turning to coat it well. Cover lightly and refrigerate, turning occasionally, for at least 24 hours and no more than 2 days.

THE TRIBECA GRILL COOKBOOK

3. Preheat and oil the grill and preheat the oven to 450°F.

4. Lift the pork from the marinade and pat it dry. Place the pork on the pre-heated grill and sear for about 4 minutes per side or until the pork is nicely browned. (Alternately, you can brown the pork in a nonstick sauté pan with a bit of oil added over medium-high heat.) Transfer the pork to a rack in a roasting pan with 1 inch of water added to the pan. Place in the preheated oven and reduce the heat to 325°F. Roast for about 1½ hours or until an instant-read thermometer inserted into the thickest part reads 170°F. Remove from the oven and allow the roast to rest for 10 minutes before slicing.

5. Slice, crosswise, into ¼-inch-thick slices. Serve immediately, with Boston Baked Beans (see page 196) and, if desired, applesauce and biscuits.

MUSHROOM-CRUSTED LOIN OF VENISON WITH BLACK PEPPER SPAETZLE

SERVES 6

I'M USUALLY PRETTY TRADITIONAL in my approach to venison—I like some type of berry sauce and some sort of spice to play off the gaminess of the meat. In this recipe, created by my German-born sous-chef, Michael Stark, the spaetzle and the lingonberries do the trick nicely.

2 cups Game Stock (see Note on page 230)
2 tablespoons unsalted butter, at room temperature
2 shallots, peeled and chopped
5 peppercorns
4 fresh thyme sprigs
1 bay leaf
1 cup port wine
2 tablespoons lingonberry preserves (see Note)
Coarse salt and freshly ground pepper to taste
Six 6-ounce venison loins (see Note)
1 tablespoon canola oil
½ recipe Mushroom Duxelles (see page 30)
⅓ cup fresh Italian-seasoned bread crumbs
1 large egg white, lightly beaten
Black Pepper Spaetzle (see page 188)

> **WINE:** The pepper in this dish is a good foil for a full-bodied, spicy Syrah from California such as Qupe Bien Nacido Reserve.

1. Place the Game Stock in a small saucepan over medium heat and bring to a boil. Lower the heat and simmer for about 15 minutes or until the stock is reduced to 1 cup. Remove from the heat and set aside.

2. Heat 1 tablespoon of the butter in a medium saucepan over medium heat. Add the shallots, peppercorns, thyme, and bay leaf and sauté for 2 minutes. Add the port wine and bring to a boil. Cook, stirring frequently, for about 15 minutes or until almost all of the liquid has evaporated. Add the reserved stock and bring to a boil. Lower the heat and barely simmer for 10 minutes. Remove from the heat and strain the sauce through a fine sieve into a clean, small saucepan. Place the sauce in the top half of a double boiler over very hot water. Add the lingonberry preserves and salt and pepper to taste. Whisk in the remaining 1 tablespoon of butter, cover lightly, and keep warm.

3. Season the venison loins with salt and pepper to taste.

4. Heat the oil in a large nonstick sauté pan over medium-high heat. Add the venison and sear for about 5 minutes, turning to brown all sides. Remove from the heat and allow to rest until cool enough to handle.

5. Preheat the oven to 450°F.

6. Combine the Mushroom Duxelles with the bread crumbs, stirring until well blended.

7. Using a pastry brush, lightly coat the cooled venison loins with the beaten egg white. Spread the mushroom mixture onto the top of the venison, pressing down to make an ⅛-inch-thick crust. Place the venison in a roasting pan in the preheated oven and roast for about 6 minutes or until an instant-read thermometer inserted into the thickest part reads 150°F for medium-rare. Remove the venison from the oven and allow to rest for about 5 minutes before carving.

8. Spoon a mound of Black Pepper Spaetzle into the center of each of six dinner plates. Using a very sharp knife, cut each loin, on the bias, into 5 slices. Fan the slices out around the spaetzle on each plate. Drizzle the Lingonberry Sauce around the edge of the plate and serve.

Accompaniments

WHIPPED POTATOES

THREE-POTATO GRATIN

YUKON SCALLION POTATOES

COCONUT RICE

BLACK PEPPER SPAETZLE

PINE NUT POLENTA

BRAISED ENDIVE

NANA'S CAPONATA

ROASTED GREEN AND YELLOW WAX BEANS
WITH HAZELNUT OIL

CARAMELIZED ONION FLAN

MOM'S STUFFED ARTICHOKES

BOSTON BAKED BEANS

MOREL AND FOIE GRAS BREAD PUDDING

WHIPPED POTATOES

SERVES 6

A LITTLE BIT RICHER and creamier than my mom's mashed potatoes, but they still serve the same purpose—the perfect accompaniment for roasts and grills, particularly with a well of gravy in the center.

6 Idaho potatoes, peeled and diced
Approximately 1 cup heavy cream
4 tablespoons unsalted butter, at room temperature
Coarse salt and freshly ground pepper to taste

1. Place the potatoes in cold, salted water to cover in a medium saucepan over high heat. Bring to a boil; lower the heat and simmer for about 20 minutes or until the potatoes are very tender. Drain well.

2. Combine the cream and butter in a small saucepan over low heat and cook to just warm the cream and melt the butter.

3. Push the drained potatoes through a potato ricer or food mill into a mixing bowl. Beat in the warm cream mixture, using just enough to make a smooth, creamy blend. Season to taste with salt and pepper and serve.

NOTE: Whipped Potatoes may be kept warm in the top half of a double boiler over very hot water.

For Peanut-Whipped Potatoes, beat ¼ cup Thai Peanut Sauce (see page 233) into the above recipe.

For additional variety, you can add ½ cup of Roasted Garlic Puree (see page 235), ½ cup pureed fresh herbs, such as basil or chives, ½ cup chopped scallions (white and green part), or ½ cup of soft cheese, such as goat or mascarpone, when you add the warm cream mixture.

THREE-POTATO GRATIN

SERVES 6

A BIT CLASSICALLY FRENCH-STYLE dauphinois and a little bit American scalloped potatoes and a lot delicious, this is not a side dish for dieters, but it is certainly worth the calories. Rich and creamy, this gratin is a great accompaniment to roast poultry, meat, or game. If desired, use just one type of potato—it will still be delicious.

¼ cup (½ stick) unsalted butter, at room temperature
2 large Idaho potatoes, peeled
2 large Yukon gold potatoes, peeled
2 large sweet potatoes, peeled
Coarse salt and freshly ground pepper to taste
1 cup milk
1 cup heavy cream
1 tablespoon Roasted Garlic Puree (see page 235)
1 tablespoon minced fresh rosemary needles
Pinch of freshly ground nutmeg
¼ teaspoon freshly ground white pepper

1. Preheat the oven to 400°F.

2. Using 2 tablespoons of the butter, generously coat an 11 by 7 by 2-inch baking pan. Set aside.

3. Cut each potato in half, lengthwise. Cut each half, crosswise, into ⅛-inch slices, keeping the halves together. Alternately place an Idaho, a Yukon gold,

NOTE: To toast ground pepper, place it in a small nonstick sauté pan over low heat. Cook, stirring constantly, for about 2 minutes or until the pepper is very aromatic but not taking on any color.

A spaetzle press or pan is available from kitchenware stores and some specialty food stores or by mail order from J. B. Prince Company (see Sources). If you don't want to purchase one, a colander with large (about ¼-inch) holes can also be used. Simply use a rubber spatula to push the dough through the holes.

PINE NUT POLENTA

SERVES 6

PINE NUTS AND MASCARPONE create perfect velvety texture and rich nuttiness.

4½ cups Vegetable Stock (see page 230) or canned vegetable broth
2 tablespoons mascarpone cheese (see Note)
2 tablespoons unsalted butter
1½ cups instant polenta (see Note)
⅓ cup toasted pine nuts
Coarse salt and freshly ground pepper to taste

1. Place the stock or broth in a medium saucepan over high heat and bring to a boil. Whisk in the cheese and butter. When melted, whisk in the polenta. Lower the heat and cook, stirring constantly with a wooden spoon, for about 5 minutes or until the polenta is quite thick but not stiff. Remove from the heat and stir in the pine nuts and salt and pepper to taste. If necessary, transfer to the top half of a double boiler over very hot water or cover with aluminum foil and place in a very low oven to keep warm until ready to use.

NOTE: Mascarpone cheese and instant polenta are available from Italian markets, specialty food stores, and some supermarkets.

Braised Endive

In America, endive is more often seen in salads than on the entrée plate. It is one of my favorite vegetables, so I am always looking for ways to introduce it onto our menu. In this recipe, I use the sweet-sour braise to soften its slightly bitter taste.

3 Belgian endives, well washed and dried
2 tablespoons unsalted butter
⅓ cup fresh orange juice
1½ tablespoons champagne or white wine vinegar

1. Preheat the oven to 375°F.

2. Cut the endives in half, lengthwise.

3. Heat the butter in a medium, ovenproof sauté pan over medium heat. Add the endives and sauté for about 5 minutes or until the endives take on some color and begin to caramelize. Add the orange juice and champagne or vinegar and stir to combine. Place in the preheated oven and bake for about 10 minutes or until tender. Remove from the oven and lightly tent to keep warm.

Nana's Caponata

SERVES 6

½ cup olive oil
1 large Spanish onion, peeled and diced
3 cloves garlic, peeled and minced
4 stalks celery, well washed and chopped
2 large eggplants, trimmed and cut into 1-inch dice
1 red bell pepper, cored, seeded, and diced
3 tablespoons tomato paste
1 teaspoon sugar
¼ cup capers, well drained
1 cup toasted pine nuts
¼ cup red wine vinegar
One 12-ounce jar Sicilian olives, drained, pitted, and chopped
Coarse salt and freshly ground pepper to taste
½ cup chopped fresh flat-leaf parsley leaves

1. Heat the oil in a large saucepan over medium heat. Add the onion and garlic and sauté for about 4 minutes or just until the onions are beginning to color. Add the celery, eggplant, and pepper and sauté for about 5 minutes or until the vegetables have wilted.

2. Stir in the tomato paste and the sugar until well combined. Stir in the capers and pine nuts. Add the vinegar and olives and bring to a simmer. Season to taste with salt and pepper and simmer, stirring occasionally, for about 15 minutes or until the vegetables are very tender and the flavors are well blended. Remove from the heat and stir in the parsley. Set aside and allow to come to room temperature. Serve at room temperature.

NOTE: Caponata will keep, covered and refrigerated, for up to 1 week. Bring to room temperature before serving.

ROASTED GREEN AND YELLOW WAX BEANS WITH HAZELNUT OIL

SERVES 6

THIS IS A VERY SIMPLE SIDE DISH in which the hazelnut oil and the roasting add interest and character to the blanched beans. Although you can use all green or all wax beans, the combination of colors does take the dish out of the ordinary.

> *½ pound fresh green beans, trimmed*
> *½ pound fresh yellow wax beans, trimmed*
> *2 tablespoons unsalted butter*
> *¼ cup hazelnut oil*
> *Coarse salt and freshly ground pepper to taste*
> *3 tablespoons toasted slivered almonds, optional*

1. Preheat the oven to 350°F.

2. Combine the beans and the butter in a medium saucepan of boiling, salted water over high heat. Return to a boil and boil for 2 minutes. Drain well and refresh under cold running water. Pat dry (see Note).

3. Place the beans in a shallow roasting pan and add the hazelnut oil, tossing to coat well. Season to taste with salt and pepper. Place in the preheated oven and roast for 8 minutes or until the beans are very tender with a touch of color. One minute before the beans are ready, if using, add the almonds and toss to combine and roast for the additional minute. Remove from the oven and serve.

NOTE: The beans can be blanched and stored, wrapped in plastic wrap and refrigerated, up to 2 days in advance.

CARAMELIZED ONION FLAN

SERVES 6

IN THIS RECIPE, the caramelized onions take the place of the usual caramel found in the traditional sweet flan of Latin countries. The flan is a lovely side dish for grilled meat, poultry, or fish, or it can also serve as an entrée served with a crisp green salad and a nice glass of crisp white wine.

5 tablespoons unsalted butter, at room temperature
1 tablespoon olive oil
2 Vidalia onions, peeled and thinly sliced
Coarse salt and freshly ground white pepper to taste
6 large eggs, beaten
6 tablespoons heavy cream
¼ cup milk

1. Using 2 tablespoons of the butter, lightly coat six 6-ounce ramekins or molds. Set aside.

2. Preheat the oven to 350°F.

3. Heat the oil in a large sauté pan over medium heat. Add the onions and season to taste with salt and pepper. Cook, stirring frequently, for 3 minutes. Add the remaining 3 tablespoons of butter and continue to cook, stirring frequently, for about 15 minutes or until the onions are very tender and beginning to caramelize. Remove from the heat and allow to cool.

4. Place the eggs, cream, and milk into a blender. Add the cooled onions and process to a smooth puree. Season to taste with salt and pepper.

5. Pour the puree into the prepared ramekins. Place the ramekins in a shallow roasting pan with cold water to cover the ramekins halfway. Place in the pre-heated oven and bake for about 25 minutes or until the flans are nicely browned and firm in the center. Remove from the oven and serve.

Mom's Stuffed Artichokes

2 cups fresh fine bread crumbs
¾ cup freshly grated Parmesan cheese
2 cloves garlic, peeled and minced
¼ cup minced fresh flat-leaf parsley leaves
Coarse salt and freshly ground pepper to taste
Juice of 1 lemon
6 medium artichokes
¾ cup olive oil

1. Combine the bread crumbs and cheese in a medium mixing bowl. Stir in the garlic and parsley. Season to taste with salt and pepper and set aside.

2. Combine the lemon juice with enough cold water to cover the cleaned artichokes in a large bowl. Set aside.

3. Working quickly with 1 artichoke at a time and using a sharp knife, cut about ¼ inch off the top of the artichoke and trim off the stem end to make a neat bottom. Using kitchen scissors, trim off the tips of each artichoke leaf. Trim off any of the lower leaves that are brown or damaged. Firmly hit the trimmed top of the artichoke against a flat surface to open the leaves slightly. Rinse the artichoke well under cold running water. Immediately place the trimmed artichoke in the acidulated water to keep it from discoloring as you trim the remaining artichokes.

4. When all of the artichokes have been trimmed and soaked, shake them, upside down, to drain out excess water. Place them, upside down, on a double thickness of paper towel to drain thoroughly. When well drained, turn the artichokes over and season lightly with salt and pepper.

5. Generously stuff the bread crumb mixture between the leaves of each artichoke. Place the stuffed artichokes into a saucepan that will hold them tightly

together (see Note). Drizzle ½ cup of the olive oil over the top of the arti-chokes and add water to the pan to come one third of the way up the sides of the artichokes. Add the remaining olive oil to the water in the pan. Cover, tightly, and place the pan over medium-high heat and bring to a boil. Immedi-ately lower the heat and gently simmer for 1½ hours or until the leaves come off very easily when pulled or until the bottom center of each artichoke is ten-der when pierced with the point of a sharp knife and the leaves can be easily removed. (If the water evaporates before the artichokes are done, add addi-tional water as needed.) Remove from the cooking liquid and allow to cool slightly before serving warm. (Alternately, allow the artichokes to come to room temperature and serve. Do not serve chilled.)

NOTE: It is sometimes helpful to use the trimmed-off stem pieces as filler in the saucepan to keep the artichokes from moving around as they cook. You can also make aluminum foil balls to use as stabilizers. Whatever you choose, you do want the artichokes to remain firmly upright as they cook.

Boston Baked Beans

SERVES 6

ALTHOUGH BAKED BEANS have always been a favorite of mine, I don't think
that I really appreciated them until I made them during a food promotion in
Tokyo. Cooks and diners alike were amazed at the depth of flavor in the pot and
were fascinated by the taste of molasses, which was totally new to them. What I
had thought of as plain home cooking became the most exotic fare and I began to
look at baked beans in a whole new way.

1 pound dried Great Northern beans, rinsed
4 whole cloves
1 large onion, peeled and quartered
2 cups water
½ cup unsulfured molasses
½ cup dark brown sugar
2 teaspoons dry mustard
1 teaspoon freshly ground pepper, plus more to taste
¼ pound salt pork
Coarse salt to taste

1. Place the beans in a large saucepan with cold water to cover by 3 inches over
   high heat. Bring to a boil and boil for 3 minutes. Immediately remove from the
   heat and allow the beans to soak for 1 hour.

2. Return the beans to medium-high heat and bring to a boil. Lower the heat and
   simmer for 20 minutes or until the beans are still slightly al dente. Remove
   from the heat and drain well.

3. Preheat the oven to 250°F.

4. Stick 1 clove into each onion quarter and place the onions in the bottom of an
   ovenproof casserole.

5. Combine the beans with the water, molasses, ¼ cup of the brown sugar, the mustard, and the pepper. Stir to blend well. Pour the beans into the casserole. Using a sharp knife, score crosshatch marks into the salt pork and push it into the center of the beans. Cover the casserole and place in the preheated oven. Bake for 4 hours.

6. Remove the casserole from the oven and uncover. Stir in salt and pepper to taste. If the beans are too dry, add up to an additional ½ cup of water. Sprinkle the top with the remaining sugar and return to the oven. Bake for about 15 minutes or until the top is lightly brown. Remove from the heat and serve.

"Probably the most exciting event at Tribeca Grill was the Artists Against Apartheid dinner honoring Nelson Mandela as he began his American goodwill tour after his release from prison. The tickets were in great demand. Security was extremely tight, with the CIA, FBI, NYPD, and military forces on guard. Three hundred very famous invited guests were carefully screened, with the most important artists in America humbly accepting this scrutiny just for the chance to see Mandela. In fact, the restaurant was silent with awestruck celebrities as Mandela entered. As he began his speech in which he told of how, although he couldn't see family and friends during his confinement, he could watch movies and sporting events, you could feel the respect mounting in the room. He continued to tell how the artists he grew to know through their movies and athletic feats became his link to the outside world and, therefore, were responsible for his survival during the long years alone. As he offered his gratitude, he caught sight of Joe Frazier and held out his hand. 'Please come join me. I was a boxer once, you know? And I just want to shake the hand of such a great man.' As Smokin' Joe approached Mandela, his face was awash with tears. And from that moment, you could hear sobs from every corner of the room. All of these people had come to honor Mandela, but he simply wanted to honor them for the gift of their art. What a night it was."

Morel and Foie Gras Bread Pudding

Serves 6

THIS IS ABOUT AS UPSCALE a bread pudding as one could create. It is very rich yet homey and is a terrific side dish for game, red meat, or squab. It could also serve as a brunch or luncheon main course with an elegant salad and a bottle of light red wine.

1 cup fresh morels, diced, or ½ cup dried morels (see Note)
3 tablespoons unsalted butter, at room temperature
2 cups heavy cream
2 shallots, peeled and minced
Coarse salt and freshly ground pepper to taste
½ cup diced foie gras (see Note)
4 cups small, fresh white bread cubes, toasted
2 large eggs
¼ teaspoon paprika
⅛ teaspoon freshly grated nutmeg
¼ teaspoon truffle oil (see Note)

1. Preheat the oven to 325°F.

2. If using dried morels, place them in a heatproof bowl with boiling water for about 30 minutes to reconstitute them. Drain well and pat dry. Dice the morels and set aside.

3. Using 2 tablespoons of the butter, generously coat an 8-inch square baking pan. Set aside.

4. Place the cream in a small saucepan over medium heat and bring to a simmer. Lower the heat and simmer for about 15 minutes or until the cream is reduced by one half, watching carefully so that the cream does not boil over. Remove from the heat and set aside.

5. Heat the remaining 1 tablespoon of butter in a medium sauté pan over medium heat. Add the shallots, morels, and salt and pepper to taste and sauté for about 3 minutes or until the shallots are tender. Remove from the heat and combine with the foie gras and toasted bread cubes. Place the mixture into the prepared loaf pan.

6. Combine the reduced cream with the eggs in a mixing bowl, whisking to blend well. Season to taste with salt and pepper. Pour the egg mixture over the morel–foie gras mixture and stir gently to combine. Sprinkle the top with paprika and nutmeg; drizzle the truffle oil over the top.

7. Tightly enclose the entire pan with aluminum foil. Place the wrapped loaf pan in a roasting pan with cold water to cover the loaf pan halfway. Place in the preheated oven and bake for 40 minutes or until the pudding is spongelike when pushed with a fingertip. Remove from the oven, unwrap, and invert onto a clean surface. Cut into ½-inch-thick slices and serve hot.

NOTE: Morels and truffle oil are available at specialty food stores.

Foie gras is available at fine-quality butchers, some specialty food stores, and by mail order from D'Artagnan (see Sources).

The pudding can be made up to 24 hours in advance. Keep wrapped in the loaf pan and reheat in a preheated 350°F oven just before serving.

MIRAMAX
99 Hudson Street • New York, New York 10013
L M S

Trailer Reel for
Peter Klein/TriBeCa guild
for British magazine group
on 14/3/99

507

Desserts

LEMON-POLENTA CAKE WITH PEACH COMPOTE

WARM PEAR AND CINNAMON FRITTERS

HOME-STYLE APPLESAUCE CAKE

TRIBECA CHOCOLATE TORTE

CARAMELIZED BANANA TART WITH MALTED
MILK–CHOCOLATE ICE CREAM

TRIBECA FILM CENTER PEANUT BUTTER PARFAIT

BUTTERMILK PANNA COTTA WITH PASSION FRUIT COULIS

LEMON-POLENTA CAKE WITH PEACH COMPOTE

MAKES ONE 10-INCH CAKE

THIS IS A VERY SIMPLE CAKE with a nice crunch and texture and a delicately sweet-tart flavor. It has some of the feel of a corn bread without the density and is best served warm.

> *1 cup (2 sticks) plus 3 tablespoons unsalted butter, at room temperature*
> *1 tablespoon all-purpose flour*
> *1⅓ cups sugar*
> *2 tablespoons freshly grated lemon zest*
> *1⅔ cups almond flour (see Note)*
> *5 large eggs*
> *1½ teaspoons pure vanilla extract*
> *1 teaspoon lemon extract*
> *⅔ cup polenta (see Note)*
> *½ cup sifted unleavened cake flour*
> *1½ teaspoons baking powder*
> *½ teaspoon coarse salt*
> *Peach Compote, optional (recipe follows)*

1. Preheat the oven to 325°F.

2. Using 1 tablespoon of the butter and the all-purpose flour, lightly coat a 10-inch cake pan. Set aside.

3. Using an electric mixer, cream together the remaining butter, the sugar, and lemon zest. When light and fluffy, beat in the almond flour and then the eggs, one at a time. Add the vanilla and lemon extracts and beat to blend.

4. Combine the polenta, cake flour, baking powder, and salt. Fold the dry mixture into the butter mixture until well blended. Pour the cake batter into the prepared

pan and place in the preheated oven. Bake for about 25 minutes or until a cake tester or toothpick inserted into the center comes out clean.

5. Remove from the oven and place on a wire rack to cool for about 20 minutes. Invert the cake onto a cake plate. Cut into wedges and serve warm with Peach Compote, if desired.

PEACH COMPOTE

MAKES ABOUT 3 CUPS

1½ pounds ripe peaches, peeled, pitted, and thinly sliced
1 teaspoon fresh lemon juice
¼ cup fresh orange juice
3 tablespoons Cointreau or other orange-flavored liqueur
3 tablespoons honey
1 teaspoon freshly grated ginger

1. Combine the peaches and lemon juice in a heatproof bowl. Set aside.

2. Combine the orange juice, Cointreau, honey, and ginger in a small nonreactive saucepan over medium heat. Bring to a boil and cook for 1 minute. Immediately pour the syrup over the peaches and stir to combine. Allow to cool for about 30 minutes. Cover and refrigerate until ready to serve.

NOTE: Almond flour and polenta are available from Italian markets, specialty food stores, and some supermarkets.

The cake may be made up to 2 days in advance and stored, tightly covered in plastic wrap and refrigerated or frozen for up to 3 months. Reheat in a very low oven before serving and, if frozen, thaw before reheating.

The lemon juice is added to the peaches to keep them from discoloring. If using other fruits, such as berries or pineapple, eliminate the lemon juice.

The compote may be made up to 3 days in advance and stored, covered and refrigerated. The same syrup may be used on fresh nectarines, apricots, berries, or pineapple.

Lemon Polenta Cake with Peach Compote (foreground); Warm Pear and Cinnamon Fritters

Warm Pear and Cinnamon Fritters

SERVES 6

THIS IS AN AMERICAN'S TAKE on the classic French wine-poached pear. It is a simple dessert with only one problem—the fritters must be made just before serving, since they must be served warm and they do not reheat well. The pears can be poached in advance and the batter made early in the day, but the whole she-bang has to come together at the last minute.

8 cups cold water
2 cups plus 3 tablespoons sugar
1 vanilla bean
1 cinnamon stick
4 firm Bartlett pears
2¼ cups plus 1 tablespoon all-purpose flour
½ teaspoon baking powder
Pinch of coarse salt
1 cup dry white wine
1 tablespoon canola oil
1 teaspoon pure vanilla extract
3 large eggs, separated
1 cup cornstarch
Approximately 4 cups vegetable oil
½ cup confectioners' sugar

1. Combine the water with 2 cups of the sugar and the vanilla bean and cinnamon stick in a large saucepan.

2. Peel the pears and remove the stems, if any. Place the peeled pears in the water mixture over high heat. Bring to a boil; lower the heat and simmer for

about 20 minutes or until the pears are tender when pierced with the point of a small, sharp knife.

3. Using a slotted spoon, remove the pears from the poaching liquid, reserving the liquid. Transfer the pears onto a plate and lightly cover with plastic wrap. Place in the refrigerator and allow to cool. Place the liquid in a nonreactive container, cover, and refrigerate.

4. When the pears are cool, cut them in half lengthwise and remove the cores. Slice each half lengthwise into 3 equal wedges. Place the wedges in the reserved poaching liquid until ready to fry. (This may be done up to 3 days in advance.)

5. Combine 1¼ cups plus 1 tablespoon of the flour with the baking powder and salt in a mixing bowl. Whisk the wine, canola oil, and vanilla extract into the flour. Add the egg yolks and whisk to blend.

6. Using an electric mixer, beat the egg whites until frothy. Add the remaining 3 tablespoons of sugar and beat until stiff peaks form. Fold the beaten egg whites into the batter. (This may be done up to 3 hours in advance.)

7. Combine the remaining flour and the cornstarch in a shallow bowl. Set aside.

8. When ready to fry, heat the vegetable oil in a deep-fat fryer or deep saucepan over high heat to 350°F on a candy thermometer.

9. Remove the pear wedges from the liquid and pat dry. One at a time, dredge the wedges into the flour-cornstarch mixture and then dip them into the batter. Place the batter-coated pear wedges into the hot oil, without crowding the pan, and fry for about 1 minute per side or until golden brown. Using a slotted spoon, lift the fritters from the oil and drain on a double thickness of paper towel. Transfer to a platter and sprinkle the fritters with the confectioners' sugar. Serve warm with vanilla ice cream or frozen yogurt, if desired.

HOME-STYLE APPLESAUCE CAKE

MAKES ONE 9-INCH SQUARE CAKE

THIS IS ANOTHER OF MY FAMILY RECIPES. Since it can be put together quickly with ingredients that are usually on hand, it is a perfect last-minute home-style dessert. It also can be put together early in the day and baked just before serving so that the house is filled with that welcoming, apples-baking aroma. At Tribeca Grill, we often use this cake as the centerpiece of a dessert buffet, as the pattern on top makes it particularly attractive.

½ cup (1 stick) plus 1 tablespoon unsalted butter, at room temperature
2 cups sifted all-purpose flour
1 cup sugar
1 teaspoon baking powder
¼ teaspoon coarse salt
1 large egg, lightly beaten
½ cup raisins, optional
½ cup walnut pieces, optional
2 cups applesauce, preferably homemade
2 Granny Smith apples, peeled, cored, and thinly sliced
3 tablespoons unsalted butter, melted
2 tablespoons cinnamon-sugar

1. Preheat the oven to 350°F.

2. Using 1 tablespoon of the butter, lightly coat a 9-inch square cake pan. Set aside.

3. Sift the flour, sugar, baking powder, and salt into a mixing bowl. Cut the remaining ½ cup of butter into the flour mixture. Add the egg and, using your hands, work the butter and egg into the flour to make a loose ball of crumbly dough. Divide the dough in half.

THE TRIBECA GRILL COOKBOOK

4. Using one half of the dough, fit the dough into the pan, pushing with your fingers to work it up the sides of the pan.

5. If using, combine the raisins and walnuts with the applesauce and pour the applesauce mixture over the dough in the pan and, using a spatula, spread it out evenly over the dough. If not using the raisins and walnuts, pour the applesauce directly over the dough.

6. Crumble the remaining dough over the applesauce, making sure that the entire top is covered. Set the apple slices over the top in a decorative pattern and, using a pastry brush, generously coat the apple slices with the melted butter. Sprinkle the top with cinnamon-sugar and place the cake in the preheated oven. Bake for 55 minutes or until the crust is golden and the apples are nicely caramelized.

7. Remove the cake from the oven and allow to cool slightly on a wire rack. Serve warm with whipped cream, ice cream, or frozen yogurt, if desired.

NOTE: The raisins and nuts are not necessary, but they do add texture and crunch to the filling.

The applesauce can be replaced with any in-season fruit. You will need 4 cups of thinly sliced fruit or whole berries mixed with 1 tablespoon sugar, 1 tablespoon all-purpose flour, 1 tablespoon lemon juice, and a pinch of cinnamon in place of the applesauce-raisin-nut mixture.

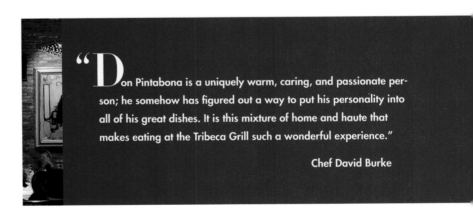

"Don Pintabona is a uniquely warm, caring, and passionate person; he somehow has figured out a way to put his personality into all of his great dishes. It is this mixture of home and haute that makes eating at the Tribeca Grill such a wonderful experience."

Chef David Burke

TRIBECA CHOCOLATE TORTE

MAKES ONE 10-INCH TORTE

THIS IS ONE OF THE TRIBECA GRILL signature desserts. It has many components and will take the good part of a day to put together. However, since many of the components can be made in advance (for instance, the mousse has to chill for at least 8 hours, and the torte has to rest at least 8 hours before cutting), it might even be a project for a couple of rainy days. The torte also keeps well, so it could also be made in advance of a special occasion and then presented as if it were just a simple exercise in home baking.

1 cup (2 sticks) plus 1 tablespoon unsalted butter,
*   at room temperature*
1 tablespoon all-purpose flour
2½ cups sugar
1 cup cocoa powder, sifted
3 large eggs
4 cups unleavened cake flour, sifted
1½ teaspoons baking powder
1½ teaspoons baking soda
1 teaspoon salt
2 cups water
½ cup slivered almonds, toasted
Dark Chocolate Custard (recipe follows)
Milk Chocolate Mousse (recipe follows)
Chocolate Ganache (recipe follows)

1. Using 1 tablespoon of the butter and the all-purpose flour, lightly coat a 10-inch springform pan.

2. Preheat the oven to 325°F.

3. In an electric mixer, cream the remaining butter and the sugar until light and fluffy. Add the cocoa and beat to blend. One at a time, add the eggs, beating to incorporate.

4. Sift together the flour, baking powder, baking soda, and salt. Alternately add the dry ingredients and water to the creamed mixture, beginning and ending with the dry ingredients.

5. Pour the batter into the prepared pan, smoothing the top with a spatula. Place in the preheated oven and bake for 20 minutes. Lower the heat to 200°F and bake for an additional 30 minutes or until a cake tester or toothpick inserted into the center comes out clean. Remove the cake from the oven and place on a wire rack to cool for 10 minutes. Remove the cake from the pan and place on a wire rack to cool completely.

6. Using a bread knife, cut a ⅛-inch-thick slice from the top of the cake. Set aside. Cut the remaining cake, crosswise, into 3 layers of equal size. Set aside.

7. Preheat the oven to 350°F.

8. Place the ⅛-inch-thick slice of cake on a baking sheet in the preheated oven and bake for about 15 minutes or until very dry. Remove from the oven and allow to cool.

9. Crumble the dried cake into the bowl of a food processor fitted with the metal blade and process, using quick on and off turns, to make fine crumbs. Combine the crumbs with the toasted almonds and set aside.

10. Place the bottom layer of cake into a 10-inch springform pan. Using a spatula, evenly spread Dark Chocolate Custard over the top, taking care not to let it run over the sides. Place the second cake layer on top of the custard. Using a spatula, evenly spread Milk Chocolate Mousse over the top, taking care not to let it run over the sides. Place the top and final layer of cake on the mousse. Using a spatula, smoothly spread a ¼-inch-thick layer of Chocolate Ganache over the top. Tightly wrap the pan in aluminum foil and refrigerate for at least 8 hours or up to 24 hours.

11. Before serving, carefully press the reserved crumb mixture around the sides of the cake, keeping the top clean. Cut into wedges and served chilled.

Dark Chocolate Custard

2 cups milk
1¼ cups sugar
6 ounces bittersweet chocolate, chopped
8 large egg yolks
½ tablespoon cornstarch

1. Combine the milk with 1 cup of the sugar in a small saucepan over medium heat. Stirring constantly, bring to a simmer. Remove from the heat.

2. Place the chocolate in the top half of a double boiler over simmering water. Heat, stirring constantly, for about 2 minutes or until the chocolate is melted. Keep the chocolate warm and melted.

3. Combine the egg yolks with the cornstarch and remaining sugar in a small bowl. Whisk vigorously to blend. Whisking constantly, slowly pour about ½ cup of the scalded milk mixture into the eggs to temper them. Whisking constantly, pour the tempered egg mixture into the scalded milk mixture in the saucepan. Return the pan to low heat and, whisking constantly, cook for about 4 minutes or until the mixture is thick and the starch taste has cooked out. Bring to a boil and continue to boil for 1 minute.

4. Pour the mixture into the bowl of an electric mixer fitted with a paddle. Add the melted chocolate and beat for about 2 minutes or until very well blended. Strain through a fine sieve into a clean bowl. Lightly cover and refrigerate for at least 2 hours or until well chilled.

MILK CHOCOLATE MOUSSE

6 tablespoons sugar
¼ cup water
1 teaspoon fresh lemon juice
3 ounces milk chocolate, chopped
2 ounces bittersweet chocolate, chopped
¼ cup (½ stick) unsalted butter, at room temperature
¾ cup heavy cream
6 tablespoons crème fraîche (see Note, page 77)
3 large egg yolks

1. Combine the sugar, water, and lemon juice in a small saucepan over medium-high heat and bring to a boil. Lower the heat and simmer for about 10 minutes or until a candy thermometer dipped into the syrup reads 252°F.

2. Combine the chocolates and butter in the top half of a double boiler over simmering water. Heat, stirring constantly, for about 2 minutes or until the chocolates melt and the butter is blended into them. Keep the chocolate warm and melted.

3. Combine the heavy cream and crème fraîche in the bowl of an electric mixer and beat until soft peaks form. Scrape the whipped cream from the mixer bowl and set aside.

4. Place the egg yolks in the mixer bowl (it is not necessary to clean it) and beat until light. With the mixer running, slowly add the hot syrup to the eggs. Add the melted chocolate and beat, on high speed, until the mixture is cool. Fold in the reserved whipped cream mixture until well blended. Scrape into a clean bowl, cover lightly, and refrigerate for at least 8 hours before using.

Chocolate Ganache

8 ounces semisweet chocolate, chopped
1 tablespoon unsalted butter, at room temperature
1 cup plus 3 tablespoons heavy cream
2 tablespoons light corn syrup

1. Combine the chocolate and butter in a small heatproof mixing bowl.

2. Place the cream and corn syrup in a small saucepan over medium heat and, stirring constantly, bring to a simmer. Immediately pour the cream mixture over the chocolate, beating until smooth. Set aside, uncovered, to cool before using. Do not cover until the ganache is cool or it will sweat and be unusable.

NOTE: Each component can be made at least a day (or up to 3 days) in advance. The cake can be put together early on the day before serving and stored, lightly covered and refrigerated.

The Dark Chocolate Custard and Milk Chocolate Mousse recipes can both be doubled for use as pudding desserts.

The Chocolate Ganache can also be used to make truffles. Simply roll the ganache into small balls and then roll the balls in cocoa powder, finely chopped nuts, or confectioners' sugar. Store, covered and refrigerated, for up to 3 days.

Caramelized Banana Tart with Malted Milk–Chocolate Ice Cream

SERVES 6

GERRY HAYDEN, TRIBECA GRILL's opening sous-chef and former pastry chef, created this now-much-copied dessert. Like many restaurant desserts, it has its share of components that can be a bit scary to the home cook. However, the cookies, the vanilla sauce, the ice cream, and the pecans can all be made in advance so the final assembly is a breeze.

> *6 large bananas*
> *6 Pecan Shortbread Cookies (recipe follows)*
> *½ cup superfine sugar*
> *Vanilla–Crème Fraîche Sauce (recipe follows)*
> *Malted Milk–Chocolate Ice Cream (recipe follows)*
> *Honey-Sugar Pecans, optional (recipe follows)*

1. Preheat the broiler.

2. Peel and thinly slice the bananas, on the bias.

3. Lay out 6 Pecan Shortbread Cookies and, working with 1 cookie at a time and starting at the center of the cookie, carefully shingle the banana slices over the cookie until the top is completely covered. When all of the cookies are covered, sprinkle the tops with sugar. Place the cookies on a cookie sheet under the preheated broiler and broil for about 2 minutes or until the bananas are caramelized.

4. Place a Caramelized Banana Tart on each of six dessert plates. Pour the Vanilla–Crème Fraîche Sauce into a plastic squeeze bottle (such as

THE TRIBECA GRILL COOKBOOK

those used for mustard and ketchup in diners) and make a circle of sauce around the edge of the plate. Place a scoop of ice cream in the center of each tart. Place 3 Honey-Sugar Pecans into the ice cream and serve.

PECAN SHORTBREAD COOKIES

1½ cups (3 sticks) unsalted butter
¾ cup sugar
1 tablespoon pure vanilla extract
3 large egg yolks, beaten
3 cups sifted all-purpose flour
1 teaspoon salt
½ cup chopped pecans

1. Preheat the oven to 375°F.

2. Line a cookie sheet with parchment paper and set aside.

3. Combine the butter, sugar, and vanilla in the bowl of an electric mixer fitted with the paddle. Beat for about 3 minutes or until well creamed. With the motor running, slowly add the egg yolks.

4. Combine the flour and salt and add it to the creamed mixture. When well combined, stir in the nuts by hand (so that the mixer will not pulverize them). Form the dough into a disk shape.

5. Place the dough on a lightly floured surface and, using a rolling pin, roll it out to about a ¼-inch thickness. Using a 4-inch round cookie or biscuit cutter, cut out 8 cookies (the extra 2 will give a breakage allowance). (Reserve the remaining dough for later use—it can be frozen, tightly wrapped—or cut it into smaller cookie shapes and bake along with the larger cookies.) Place the cookies on the prepared cookie sheet in the preheated oven and bake for 15 minutes or until golden. Remove from the oven and cool on a wire rack.

Vanilla–Crème Fraîche Sauce

1 cup heavy cream
2 tablespoons sugar
½ vanilla bean, split open
¾ cup crème fraîche (see Note, page 77)

1. Combine the cream, sugar, and vanilla bean in a small saucepan over medium heat. Bring to a boil; immediately remove from the heat. Watch carefully, as cream will boil over quickly. Set aside to cool. Remove the vanilla bean before using.

2. Whisk the crème fraîche into the cooled cream mixture. Cover and refrigerate for up to 3 days.

Malted Milk–Chocolate Ice Cream

4 cups milk
1¼ cups heavy cream
5 tablespoons sugar
5 large egg yolks, beaten
1 pound milk chocolate, chopped
¾ cup barley malt syrup (see Note)
1 cup coarsely chopped toasted walnuts

1. Combine the milk, cream, and sugar in a medium saucepan over medium heat. Cook, stirring frequently, until the mixture just reaches a simmer. Immediately remove from the heat.

2. Place the eggs in a small, heatproof bowl and slowly whisk about 1 cup of the hot milk mixture into them to temper. Once combined, slowly whisk the egg mixture into the hot milk mixture in the saucepan. Whisk vigorously to blend well.

3. Whisk the chocolate into the hot milk mixture. When melted, whisk in the barley malt.

4. Place the saucepan in a bowl of ice water and, stirring frequently, allow the mixture to cool.

5. When cool, stir in the nuts and place in an ice cream maker and freeze according to the manufacturer's directions.

HONEY-SUGAR PECANS

1 cup pecan halves
½ cup honey
½ cup confectioners' sugar

1. Preheat the oven to 200°F.

2. Toss the pecans and honey together. Place the nuts in a single layer on a cookie sheet in the preheated oven. Bake for about 20 minutes or until dry.

3. Remove from the oven and place in a mixing bowl. Toss with the sugar until well coated. Store, tightly covered, for up to 2 weeks.

NOTE: Barley malt syrup is available from health food stores and bakery supply houses.

TRIBECA FILM CENTER PEANUT BUTTER PARFAIT

SERVES 6

WHEN I WAS DOING an American food promotion in Asia, one of the Malaysian pastry cooks wanted to play with some of my American ingredients. He was particularly taken with peanut butter, from which he created this recipe. It was so good that I had to ask for the recipe to bring back to the restaurant. Garnished with chocolate "film strips," it became a signature dessert honoring our upstairs neighbors. This dessert is a bit complicated, but since the parfait needs to chill at least 8 hours, it can be prepared the day before serving.

> *1 teaspoon unflavored gelatin*
> *2 tablespoons water*
> *3 cups plus 2 tablespoons heavy cream*
> *10 ounces white chocolate, finely chopped*
> *1½ cups smooth peanut butter*
> *4 large eggs, beaten*
> *Sponge Cake (recipe follows)*
> *Chocolate Ganache, warmed (see page 246)*
> *1 cup fresh raspberries*
> *6 sprigs of fresh mint*

1. Combine the gelatin and water in a small saucepan and let sit for about 3 minutes. Place over low heat and cook, stirring constantly, just until the gelatin is dissolved. Set aside.

2. Place 1 cup plus 2 tablespoons of the heavy cream in a medium saucepan over medium heat. Bring to a simmer. Immediately add the chocolate and remove from the heat. Stir constantly until the chocolate melts. Add the peanut butter and reserved gelatin and whisk to combine. Whisk in the eggs until well blended. Set aside to cool.

3. When the mixture is cool, beat the remaining heavy cream until soft peaks form. Carefully fold the whipped cream into the peanut butter mixture and set aside.

4. Cut six 2½-inch circles from the Sponge Cake. Fit each circle into the bottom of a 2½-inch soufflé dish. Pour the peanut butter mixture into each dish to come up to the top. Smooth the top with a spatula. Cover with plastic wrap and refrigerate for at least 8 hours or overnight.

5. Remove the chilled parfaits from the soufflé dishes (you might have to wrap the dish in a very hot towel to loosen the mold). Place the parfaits on a wire rack. Carefully pour the warm Chocolate Ganache over the parfaits, allowing it to randomly run down the sides. Return the parfaits to the refrigerator for at least 30 minutes to allow the ganache to harden.

6. Serve chilled with fresh raspberries around the edge of the plate and a sprig of mint in the top.

SPONGE CAKE

2 tablespoons unsalted butter
2 tablespoons Wondra flour (see Note, page 69)
2 large egg whites
Pinch of cream of tartar
½ cup plus 1 tablespoon sugar
2 large eggs
2 large egg yolks
¾ cup plus 1 tablespoon sifted all-purpose flour
2 tablespoons unsalted butter, melted
1 teaspoon pure vanilla extract

1. Preheat the oven to 350°F.

2. Using the 2 tablespoons of butter and Wondra flour, generously coat a 10-inch round cake pan. Set aside.

3. Combine the egg whites with the cream of tartar and, using an electric mixer, beat the whites until stiff peaks form. Set aside.

4. Combine the sugar, whole eggs, and egg yolks in a heatproof bowl and whisk vigorously to combine. Place the bowl in very hot water and, whisking constantly, beat the mixture until it reaches 86°F on an instant-read thermometer. Transfer the warm mixture to the bowl of an electric mixer and beat, using the balloon whisk, until the mixture has doubled in volume. Continue beating on medium for about 10 minutes or until the mixture is cool and forms a ribbon when lifted from the bowl.

5. Sift the flour over the egg mixture and, using a large, flat, slotted spoon, gently fold it in, taking care not to overwork the batter. Fold in the butter and vanilla. When incorporated, carefully fold in the reserved beaten egg whites.

6. Pour the batter into the prepared pan and place in the preheated oven. Bake for 15 minutes or until golden and a cake tester or toothpick inserted into the center comes out clean. Remove from the oven and invert the cake onto a wire rack or clean cookie sheet (to keep it from sticking in the pan) to cool. Store, covered, for up to 1 day.

NOTE: Since only a portion of the Sponge Cake is used for the parfaits, the remainder can be tightly wrapped and frozen for up to 3 months.

Buttermilk Panna Cotta with Passion Fruit Coulis

SERVES 6

"PANNA COTTA" OR "COOKED CREAM" is a traditional home-style Italian dessert. In this recipe, the tartness of the buttermilk serves to accent the richness of the cream in this easy-to-make but quite delicious pudding.

> *1½ tablespoons unflavored gelatin*
> *1 cup plus 3 tablespoons water*
> *1 cup buttermilk*
> *4 cups heavy cream*
> *1¼ cups sugar*
> *1 vanilla bean, cut in half crosswise*
> *3 ripe passion fruit*
> *One 12-ounce can pitted apricots, drained and pureed*
> *6 sprigs of fresh mint*

1. Lightly coat six 6-ounce molds with nonstick vegetable spray. Set aside.

2. Combine the gelatin with 3 tablespoons of the water in a small saucepan and let sit for 3 minutes. Place over low heat and cook, stirring constantly, just until the gelatin dissolves. Remove from the heat and stir in the buttermilk. Set aside.

3. Combine the cream and ¾ cup of the sugar in a medium saucepan. Split open one half of the vanilla bean and scrape the seeds into the cream mixture. Add the split bean to the mixture and bring to a boil. Immediately, whisk in the reserved buttermilk mixture and return to a simmer. Remove from the heat and strain through a fine sieve into the prepared molds. Cover lightly with plastic wrap and refrigerate for at least 8 hours or overnight.

4. Combine the remaining ½ cup of sugar with the remaining 1 cup of water and vanilla bean half in a small saucepan over high heat. Bring to a boil. Lower the heat and simmer for 10 minutes. Remove from the heat and allow to cool (see Note).

5. Peel the passion fruit and cut them in half crosswise. Using a teaspoon, scoop out the seeds and place the fruit in a small bowl. Add the apricot puree and ½ cup of the reserved vanilla syrup and stir until well blended. Cover and refrigerate until ready to serve.

6. Place a pool of the Passion Fruit Coulis in the center of each of six dessert plates. Unmold a panna cotta into the center of each plate. Garnish with a mint sprig and serve.

NOTE: Panna cotta will keep, covered and refrigerated, for up to 3 days.

The vanilla syrup is a basic simple syrup that will keep, covered and refrigerated, for up to 6 months. It can be used to flavor drinks, sweeten fruit sorbets, or to dilute liqueurs.

Tribeca Basics

A WORD ABOUT STOCKS, BROTHS, AND COURT BOUILLON

CHICKEN (OR BROWN CHICKEN) STOCK

VEAL STOCK

VEGETABLE STOCK

COURT BOUILLON

VINAIGRETTES AND SAUCES

LEMON-CAPER VINAIGRETTE

BALSAMIC VINAIGRETTE

CITRUS VINAIGRETTE

WALNUT VINAIGRETTE

SESAME VINAIGRETTE

GINGER-SOY DIPPING SAUCE

SWEET AND SOUR SAUCE

THAI PEANUT SAUCE

GARLIC-ANCHOVY AÏOLI

SPICY RÉMOULADE

BEURRE BLANC

MARINIÈRE

NATURAL JUS

SEASONINGS

BOUQUET GARNI

OILS AND FONDUES

GARLIC OIL AND ROASTED GARLIC PUREE

BASIL OIL

LEMON OIL

TOMATO OIL AND TOMATO FONDUE

PICKLES AND PRESERVES

PRESERVED MUSHROOMS

PICKLED ONIONS

PICKLED JAPANESE EGGPLANT

CURED LEMONS OR LEMON CONFIT

ROASTED RED PEPPERS

OVEN-DRIED TOMATOES

SPICED WALNUTS

MEATS

DUCK CONFIT

MOM'S MEATBALLS

BRAISED OXTAILS

DOUGH

PASTA DOUGH

A WORD ABOUT WINE

DESSERT WINES

A WORD ABOUT STOCKS, BROTHS, AND COURT BOUILLON

ALMOST EVERY RESTAURANT or chef's cookbook will offer a recipe for chicken, veal, and vegetable stock, which, of course, are standard everyday items in a restaurant kitchen. In fact, it would be impossible to build the richly flavored sauces of the restaurant repertoire without the backbone of a rich stock. However, I don't know any chef who would make a fresh stock for home use. Certainly, a stock often gets carried home from the restaurant kitchen for a special home-cooked meal, but I would bet that, just as often, a can of commercially prepared broth is what is used.

There is no denying that a homemade stock, be it chicken, veal, meat, game, vegetable, or mushroom, will add a depth of flavor to a sauce, soup, or stew that cannot be achieved with canned broths. But we do have to be realistic about the time constraints of most home cooks. When cooking at home, we usually work without the luxury of the hours necessary to create a stock (unless brewing up a great stock is your idea of relaxing weekend activity), so canned broth is what is usually on hand. If this is your case, use it and don't feel guilty.

If you have homemade stock available, by all means use it in any of my recipes calling for stock or broth. If you don't and you want to make a batch, I have included my recipes.

Of the brands of canned broths on the market, I highly recommend Pacific Natural broths. They are all-natural organic chicken, vegetable, and mushroom cooking broths (for information, call 503-692-9666) that are sold in health food and specialty food stores as well as some supermarkets. Campbell's Healthy Request, which is sold at almost every supermarket, is another good choice. To create a veal-type broth, combine two-thirds chicken broth with one-third beef broth. It certainly won't be equal to a restaurant veal stock, but it will work just fine in a pinch.

CHICKEN STOCK

MAKES ABOUT 8 CUPS

4 pounds chicken carcasses and/or necks and backs
1 tablespoon canola oil
3 medium carrots, peeled and chopped
2 cups chopped onions
2 cups chopped celery
1½ teaspoons dried thyme
8 peppercorns
1 bay leaf
1 gallon water

1. Rinse the chicken bones and pieces. Pat dry and set aside.

2. Heat the oil in a large stockpot over medium heat. Add the carrots, onions, and celery and cook, stirring frequently, for about 5 minutes or until the vegetables are just soft. Stir in the chicken carcass and/or pieces, thyme, peppercorns, and bay leaf. When well combined, add the water. Bring to a boil; lower the heat and simmer, occasionally skimming off the scum that floats on top, for about 1½ hours or until the liquid is reduced to 8 cups.

3. Strain through a fine sieve into a storage container, pushing on the solids to extract as much liquid as possible. Discard the solids. Allow the stock to cool slightly, spooning off the fat as it rises to the surface. Cover and refrigerate for up to 3 days or freeze, in small quantities for ease of use, for up to 3 months. Before using, spoon or scrape off any fat that has solidified on top.

NOTE: For Brown Chicken Stock, roast the chicken carcasses and pieces in a preheated 350°F oven for about 15 minutes before adding

them to the stock. If you want to create the deeply rich stocks used at Tribeca Grill, replace all water used with stock or even canned chicken broth.

VEAL STOCK

MAKES ABOUT 6 CUPS

7 pounds veal knuckle
  and marrow bones
¼ cup plus 2 tablespoons
  vegetable oil
3 onions, peeled and chopped
2 carrots, peeled and chopped
1 cup chopped celery
1 gallon water
1 cup canned tomato puree
1½ teaspoons dried thyme
8 peppercorns
1 bay leaf

1. Preheat the oven to 350°F.

2. Using ¼ cup of the oil, lightly coat the bones. Place the bones in a roasting pan in the preheated oven and roast, turning occasionally, for about 20 minutes or until well browned. Using a slotted spoon, transfer the bones to a large stockpot.

3. If necessary, add the remaining oil to the roasting pan. Stir in the onions, carrots, and celery and place the pan over medium heat on top of the stove. Cook, stirring frequently, for about 5 minutes or until the vegetables are soft. Using a slotted spoon, transfer the vegetables to the stockpot.

4. Pour the fat from the roasting pan. Add 2 cups of water and return the pan to medium heat on top of the stove. Cook, stirring constantly, scraping up any particles sticking to the bottom of the pan, for about 2 minutes or until the pan is deglazed. Pour the liquid into the stockpot. Add the remaining water, along with the tomato puree, thyme, peppercorns, and bay leaf and stir to combine. Place over medium-high heat and bring to a boil. Lower the heat and simmer, occasionally skimming off the foam and fat, for about 3 hours or until the liquid is reduced to about 6 cups. Strain through a very fine sieve, pushing on the solids to extract as much liquid as possible. Discard the solids. Allow the strained liquid to cool slightly, spooning off fat as it rises to the top. Cover and refrigerate for up to 3 days or freeze, in small quantities for ease of use, for up to 3 months. Before using, spoon or scrape off any fat that has solidified on top.

NOTE: Use beef, lamb, or game bones in place of the veal bones and follow this basic recipe for beef, lamb, or game stock.

VEGETABLE STOCK

MAKES 4 CUPS

2 tablespoons olive oil
8 cloves garlic, peeled and
  chopped
6 large mushrooms, cleaned
  and chopped
3 stalks celery, well washed
  and chopped
2 large carrots, peeled,
  trimmed,
  and chopped
2 large onions, peeled and
  chopped
2 large tomatoes, well washed,
  cored, and chopped
2 large bell peppers, well
  washed, cored, seeded, and
  chopped
1 Bouquet Garni (see page 235)
½ cup white wine
6 cups water

Heat the olive oil in a large saucepan over medium heat. Add the garlic, mushrooms, celery, carrots, onions, tomatoes, and bell peppers. Sauté for 5 minutes or until the vegetables are soft. Add the Bouquet Garni and wine and cook, stirring constantly, for 1 minute to deglaze the pan. Raise the heat and add the water. Bring to a boil. Immediately, lower the heat and simmer for 45 minutes or until the liquid is reduced to 4 cups. Strain through a fine sieve, pushing on the solids to extract as much liquid as possible, discarding the solids. Pour the stock into a nonreactive container and store, tightly covered and refrigerated, for up to 2 days or frozen for up to 3 months.

NOTE: Almost any vegetable can be used to make stock; even vegetable trimmings can be added to the pot for extra flavor. Stronger-

flavored vegetables, like turnips or broccoli, are not recommended, as they will overpower the softer flavors and make a very strong stock.

COURT BOUILLON

MAKES 4 CUPS

COURT BOUILLON is a lightly aromatic liquid used to poach poultry, white meats, seafood, or vegetables. It is generally used when you want to cook something that does not require intense flavor for a very short period of time ("court" translates as "short" in English). When poaching poultry, white meat, or fish, it is important that the court bouillon have some acid, such as wine, vinegar, or citrus juice, to firm the flesh as it cooks. Shellfish, small pieces of fish, chicken breast halves or thighs, or vegetables (whole or in pieces) may be poached as is. Large pieces of poultry or meat (such as turkey breasts or tenderloins) or fish (such as a whole fish) will hold their shape better if tied with kitchen twine or wrapped in cheesecloth. The liquid should barely cover the item to be poached and it should just gently simmer as it poaches.

This is a very basic poaching liquid that we use in the Tribeca kitchen. It is enough for about 2 pounds of meat or fish and it can easily be doubled. If you don't need an infusion of saltiness into the item to be poached, do not add salt. If you require a more aromatic liquid, you can add a Bouquet Garni or some sprigs of fresh herbs, a couple of cloves of garlic, and/or some citrus peels.

> *4 cups cold water*
> *1 cup dry white wine*
> *1 large onion, peeled and chopped*
> *1 carrot, peeled, trimmed, and chopped*
> *1 stalk celery, peeled and chopped*
> *5 peppercorns*
> *1 bay leaf*
> *Coarse salt to taste, optional*

Combine the water and wine in a saucepan over medium-high heat. Stir in the onion, carrot, celery, peppercorns, bay leaf, and, if using, salt. Bring to a boil. Add the item(s) to be poached and return to a very gentle simmer. Simmer until just cooked through. Do not overcook or the vegetables will get mushy and the poultry, meat, or seafood will toughen. Shrimp will take about 1 to 2 minutes, depending upon their size; fish steaks or boneless fillets will take from 2 minutes to 5 minutes, depending

on the degree of thickness; whole fish will take about 10 minutes; chicken breast halves will take about 7 minutes; pork tenderloin will take about 10 minutes. You can also use an instant-read thermometer to gauge the required degree of doneness for the item you are poaching.

VINAIGRETTES AND SAUCES

LEMON-CAPER VINAIGRETTE

> *Makes about 3 cups*
> *¼ cup soy sauce*
> *2 tablespoons red wine vinegar*
> *2 tablespoons white wine vinegar*
> *1 teaspoon sambal olek (chunky Thai chili paste) (see Note, page 233)*
> *Juice and zest of 1 lemon*
> *Juice and zest of 1 lime*
> *1 cup olive oil*
> *2 shallots, peeled and finely diced*
> *1 red bell pepper, cored, seeded, and cut into fine dice*
> *¼ cup chopped mixed herbs (see Note)*
> *2 tablespoons minced capers, well drained*
> *1 tablespoon minced fresh ginger*
> *Coarse salt and freshly ground pepper to taste*

Combine the soy sauce, red and white wine vinegars, and sambal olek in a small mixing bowl. Whisk in the juice and zest of the lemon and lime. When well blended, slowly whisk in the olive oil. This is not an emulsified vinaigrette, so don't worry if it does not hold together. Blend in the shallots, bell pepper, herbs, capers, and ginger. Taste and adjust the seasoning with salt and pepper. Use immediately or store, covered and refrigerated, for up to 3 days.

NOTE: The herbs used in this vinaigrette are based on the flavors required to either balance or highlight a specific dish. If you are unsure of the balance you are trying to achieve, the classic French mixture known as fines herbes, equal portions of fresh flat-leaf parsley, chervil, chives, and tarragon, will create a safe starting point. I will often replace the chervil and tarragon with cilantro and basil for seafood or pork dishes and I encourage you to experiment to find the flavor combinations that you like best.

BALSAMIC VINAIGRETTE

MAKES ABOUT 1¹/2 CUPS

½ cup balsamic vinegar
2 teaspoons minced niçoise olives
½ cup olive oil

½ cup Garlic Oil (see page 235)
Coarse salt and freshly ground pepper to taste

Combine the vinegar and olives in a small bowl. Slowly whisk in the olive oil and Garlic Oil until well emulsified. Season to taste with salt and pepper. Store, covered, at room temperature, for up to 3 days.

CITRUS VINAIGRETTE

MAKES ABOUT 1³/4 CUPS

6 tablespoons fresh lemon juice
3 tablespoons honey
1 cup olive oil
2 tablespoons fresh lemon thyme leaves
Coarse salt and freshly ground pepper to taste

Whisk together the lemon juice and honey in a small bowl. When well combined, slowly whisk in the oil until well emulsified. Add the lemon thyme and salt and pepper to taste. Cover and refrigerate for up to 3 days.

WALNUT VINAIGRETTE

MAKES ABOUT 1¹/2 CUPS

3 tablespoons red wine vinegar
2 teaspoons Dijon mustard
1 cup walnut oil (see Note)
¼ cup blended olive oil
Coarse salt and freshly ground pepper to taste

Combine the vinegar and Dijon mustard in a small bowl. Slowly add the walnut and blended oils and whisk together until well emulsified. Season to taste with salt and pepper. Store, covered and refrigerated, for up to 1 week.

NOTE: Walnut oil is available from specialty food stores and some health food stores.

SESAME VINAIGRETTE

MAKES ABOUT 2 CUPS

¼ cup sherry wine vinegar
¼ teaspoon soy sauce
1 teaspoon Dijon mustard
1 cup hazelnut oil (see Note)
6 tablespoons canola oil
1 teaspoon sesame oil (see Note)
Coarse salt and freshly ground pepper to taste

Combine the vinegar and soy sauce in a small bowl. Whisk in the mustard. When well combined, slowly whisk in the hazelnut, canola, and sesame oils until well emulsified. Season to taste with salt and pepper. Store, covered and refrigerated, for up to 1 week.

NOTE: Hazelnut and sesame oils are available from specialty food stores and some health food stores.

Ginger-Soy Dipping Sauce

MAKES ABOUT 1 1/2 CUPS

3/4 cup soy sauce

1/3 cup plus 2 tablespoons water

1 tablespoon sake (see Note, page 48)

1 tablespoon mirin (Japanese rice wine) (see Note, page 48)

1 tablespoon sugar

2 1/2 teaspoons minced fresh ginger

1 clove garlic, peeled and minced

1/4 teaspoon dried crushed red pepper

Combine the soy sauce, water, sake, and mirin in a small nonreactive container. Whisk in the sugar. When the sugar has dissolved, stir in the ginger, garlic, and crushed red pepper. Cover and refrigerate for up to 1 week.

Sweet and Sour Sauce

MAKES ABOUT 2 CUPS

1 tablespoon hijiki seaweed (see Note)

2 cups sugar

1 1/4 cups rice wine vinegar (see Note)

1/2 cup water

1 tablespoon nam pla (Thai fish sauce) (see Note)

1/2 teaspoon sambal olek (chunky Thai chili paste) (see Note)

1/2 teaspoon minced garlic

1 large mango, peeled and finely diced

2 tablespoons finely diced red bell pepper

1. Place the hijiki in warm water to cover by 2 inches and soak for 30 minutes. Drain well and set aside.

2. Combine the sugar, vinegar, and water in a medium heavy-bottomed saucepan over medium heat. Bring to a boil; lower the heat and simmer for about 15 minutes or until the liquid has reduced slightly and turned golden brown as it begins to caramelize. Immediately stir in the nam pla, sambal olek, and garlic. Return to the simmer and cook, simmering gently, for about 2 minutes or until the mixture has thickened slightly. Remove from the heat and allow to cool.

3. When the mixture has cooled, stir in the mango, bell pepper, and the reserved hijiki. If not serving immediately, cover and refrigerate for up to 3 days. Serve at room temperature.

NOTE: Hijiki, rice wine vinegar, nam pla, and sambal olek are available at Asian markets and some specialty food stores.

Thai Peanut Sauce

MAKES ABOUT 1/2 CUP

1 teaspoon peanut oil

2 tablespoons minced shallots

1 teaspoon minced garlic

1 teaspoon Thai red curry paste (see Note)

1 cup canned coconut milk

1/4 cup finely chopped unsalted peanuts

1 tablespoon nam pla (Thai fish sauce) (see Note)

1 teaspoon honey

Pinch of curry powder

Coarse salt and freshly ground pepper to taste

1. Heat the oil in a medium saucepan over medium heat. Add the shallots, garlic, and curry paste and cook, stirring frequently, for 4 minutes. Add the coconut milk, peanuts, fish sauce, honey, and curry powder and bring to a boil. Immediately lower the heat and simmer for about 10 minutes or until the mixture is reduced by one half.

2. Pour the reduced sauce into a blender and process to a smooth puree. Taste and adjust the seasoning with salt and pepper. Serve at room temperature.

NOTE: Thai red curry paste and nam pla are available at Asian markets and specialty food stores.

Thai Peanut Sauce may be stored, covered and refrigerated, for up to 3 days or frozen for up to 6 months. Bring to room temperature before using.

GARLIC-ANCHOVY AÏOLI

MAKES ABOUT 2 CUPS

2 large eggs, beaten
2 tablespoons rice wine vinegar (see Note, page 233)
3 anchovy fillets, well drained and minced
½ teaspoon minced garlic
½ teaspoon turmeric
1½ cups peanut oil
Coarse salt and freshly ground pepper to taste

Place the eggs and vinegar in a mixing bowl and whisk vigorously to combine. (If you are concerned about the safety of eating uncooked eggs, replace the above ingredients and the peanut oil with 1½ cups fine-quality mayonnaise, which can be seasoned with the anchovies, garlic, and turmeric.) Add the anchovies, garlic, and turmeric and whisk to blend. Slowly whisk in the oil, beating until the mixture is the consistency of mayonnaise. Taste and adjust the seasoning with salt and pepper. Store, covered and refrigerated, for up to 3 days.

NOTE: Aïoli emulsifies best when done in a food processor fitted with

a metal blade, but since this is such a small amount, it is difficult to work in a large food processor. If you have a small food processor or a large food processor fitted with a small bowl attachment, use it for ease and great results.

SPICY RÉMOULADE

MAKES ABOUT 3 CUPS

1 cup fine-quality mayonnaise
3 tablespoons chopped fresh flat-leaf parsley
3 tablespoons minced capers
½ tablespoon prepared horseradish, well drained
1 tablespoon sriracha (smooth Thai chili paste) (see Note)
Coarse salt and freshly ground pepper to taste

Combine the mayonnaise with the parsley, capers, horseradish, and sriracha in a small bowl. Taste and adjust the seasoning with salt and pepper. Store, covered and refrigerated, for up to 3 days.

NOTE: Sriracha is available from Asian markets and some specialty food stores.

BEURRE BLANC

MAKES ABOUT 1 CUP

1 teaspoon canola oil
2 shallots, peeled and chopped
1 cup dry white wine
¼ cup white wine vinegar
6 white peppercorns
1 bay leaf

1 cup (2 sticks) unsalted butter, cubed and at room temperature
Coarse salt and freshly ground pepper to taste

Heat the oil in a small saucepan over medium heat. Add the shallots and sauté for about 4 minutes or until the shallots are soft but have not taken on any color. Add the wine, vinegar, peppercorns, and bay leaf and cook, stirring occasionally, for about 12 minutes or until the pan is almost dry. Begin whisking in the butter, a little at a time, until it is well incorporated and the sauce is slightly thick. Strain through a fine sieve into the top half of a double boiler over very hot water to keep warm until serving. Season to taste with salt and pepper.

NOTE: If not handled carefully, Beurre Blanc can separate. If it does, whisk in a couple of tablespoons of butter, whisking until the sauce comes together.

MARINIÈRE

MAKES ABOUT ⅓ CUP

¼ cup olive oil
2 tablespoons finely diced shallots
2 tablespoons finely diced garlic
2 tablespoons tomato paste
1 teaspoon fresh lemon juice
1 teaspoon white wine
½ teaspoon white wine vinegar
½ bay leaf

*Coarse salt and freshly ground
pepper*

1. Combine the oil, shallots, and
garlic in a small sauté pan over
medium heat. Cook, stirring frequently, for about 2 minutes or
until the vegetables are soft and
the mixture is very fragrant.

2. Add the tomato paste, lemon
juice, wine, vinegar, and bay leaf
and stir to combine. Add salt and
pepper to taste and bring to a boil.
Lower the heat and, stirring frequently, simmer gently for 7 minutes. Remove from the heat and
serve warm. Alternatively, store,
covered and refrigerated, for up to
1 week. Reheat before using.

Natural Jus

Makes about 1 cup

*3 cups Veal, Lamb, or Game
    Stock (see page 230)
2 tablespoons olive oil
2 shallots, peeled and chopped
3 tablespoons chopped flat-leaf
    parsley
5 peppercorns
1 bay leaf
1 cup dry red wine
Coarse salt and freshly ground
    pepper to taste*

1. Place the stock in a medium
saucepan over medium heat and
bring to a boil. Lower the heat and
simmer for about 30 minutes or
until reduced to 1 cup. Remove
from the heat and set aside.

2. Place the oil in a medium
saucepan over medium heat. Add
the shallots, parsley, peppercorns,
and bay leaf and sauté for about 3
minutes or until the shallots are
soft. Add the red wine and cook,
stirring frequently, for about 15
minutes or until the pan is almost
dry. Stir in the reserved reduced
stock and bring to a simmer. Add
salt and pepper to taste and simmer for about 5 minutes. Strain
through a fine sieve into a clean
saucepan. Place over low heat
and bring to a simmer. Serve or
place in the top half of a double
boiler over very hot water until
ready to serve.

NOTE: Use whatever stock com-
plements the meat used in the
recipe calling for Natural Jus. For
instance, if you are going to use a
Natural Jus with a rack of lamb,
you will need to use reduced lamb
stock to make the Natural Jus.

SEASONINGS

Bouquet Garni

Bouquet garni, a group of
herbs tied together or placed in a
cheesecloth bag, is used to flavor
sauces, soups, or stews. The
tying or bagging facilitates their
easy removal from the pot. The
traditional mix is parsley, thyme,
and bay leaf. When my recipes
call for a bouquet garni, you will

need 12 parsley stems, 10 peppercorns, 1 teaspoon dried
thyme, and 2 bay leaves tied in a
cheesecloth bag.

OILS AND FONDUES

Garlic Oil and Roasted Garlic Puree

Makes 2 cups

*2 heads garlic, cut in half
    crosswise
2 cups olive oil*

1. Preheat the oven to 250°F.

2. Combine the garlic and oil in a
small roasting pan. Tightly wrap and
seal the entire pan with aluminum
foil. Poke five tiny holes in the top of
the foil. Place the pan in the preheated oven and roast for about 1½
hours or until the garlic is deeply
aromatic and very soft and the oil is
golden brown. Remove from the
oven and strain the oil through a fine
sieve into a clean container (see
Note). Cover and store, at room temperature, for up to 1 week.

NOTE: If you would like to make
Roasted Garlic Puree, which is a
great flavoring for sauces, soups,
and braises, as well as a great spread
for crusty, peasant-style breads,
roast 4 whole heads of garlic as
above but instead of discarding the
garlic when it has cooled, push the

garlic through a food mill or squeeze the soft, buttery garlic from the skins into a storage container. Cover and refrigerate for up to 3 days or freeze for up to 6 months.

BASIL OIL

MAKES ABOUT 1¼ CUPS

1 large bunch of fresh basil, well washed and dried
½ cup canola oil
½ cup olive oil
Coarse salt and freshly ground pepper to taste

1. Place the basil in boiling salted water for 15 seconds. Drain well and refresh under cold running water until well chilled. Drain well, pat dry, and chop.

2. Pour the canola and olive oils into a blender. With the motor running, add the chopped basil and salt and pepper to taste. Blend until smooth. Pour into a nonreactive container. Cover and refrigerate for up to 3 days.

NOTE: Mint Oil can be made in this same way, substituting fresh mint for the basil.

LEMON OIL

MAKES 2 CUPS

2 cups blended olive oil
Rinds of 6 lemons (see Note)
4 sprigs of fresh thyme

Combine the oil, lemon rinds, and thyme in a medium saucepan over medium heat. Bring to just a simmer; immediately turn down the heat to the lowest possible setting and cook for 30 minutes. Do not boil or simmer. Remove from the heat and allow to cool. Strain through a fine sieve into a clean nonreactive container and store, covered and refrigerated, for up to 1 month.

NOTE: At Tribeca Grill, we use the rinds of lemons that we have used for juice. Make sure that there is no juice left in the rinds or the oil will separate and be unusable.

TOMATO OIL AND TOMATO FONDUE

MAKES ABOUT 1 CUP OIL AND ¾ CUP FONDUE

½ cup plus 2 tablespoons olive oil
3 shallots, peeled and minced
1 tablespoon minced garlic
2 cups tomato paste
½ cup canola oil
Coarse salt and freshly ground pepper to taste

1. Heat 2 tablespoons of the olive oil in a small saucepan over medium heat. Add the shallots and garlic and sauté for about 3 minutes or until the vegetables are golden. Stir in the tomato paste and, when well combined, stir in the canola oil and the remaining

olive oil. Lower the heat and simmer for 12 minutes. Season to taste with salt and pepper.

2. Strain the oil through a very fine sieve into a clean container, reserving the solids (the fondue). Cover the oil and store, at room temperature, for up to 3 days.

3. Place the fondue into a cheesecloth bag. Twist the ends together to squeeze out any excess liquid. Place the fondue in a nonreactive container and store, covered and refrigerated, for up to 1 week.

PICKLES AND PRESERVES

PRESERVED MUSHROOMS

MAKES 1 POUND

1 pound shiitake mushrooms, brushed clean and stems removed
½ cup rice wine vinegar (see Note)
½ cup sake (see Note, page 48)
½ cup mirin (see Note)
¼ cup soy sauce
1 tablespoon sugar
½ teaspoon hon dashi (powdered fish stock) (see Note)
Coarse salt and freshly ground pepper to taste

Cut the mushrooms into a fine julienne and place them in a

medium, nonreactive saucepan. Stir in the vinegar, sake, mirin, and soy sauce. Add the sugar and dashi and enough water to cover the mushrooms. Place over medium-high heat and bring to a boil. Lower the heat and simmer for about 30 minutes or until the liquid has evaporated. Remove from the heat and season to taste with salt and pepper. Store, covered and refrigerated, for up to 3 days.

NOTE: Rice wine vinegar, mirin, and dashi are available from Asian markets, specialty food stores, and some supermarkets and health food stores.

PICKLED ONIONS

MAKES ABOUT 3 CUPS

½ cup rice wine vinegar
  (see Note above)
½ cup water
¼ cup sugar
1 tablespoon juniper berries
2 large red onions, peeled and
  sliced paper-thin, crosswise

Combine the vinegar, water, sugar, and juniper berries in a medium nonreactive saucepan over high heat. Bring to a boil; immediately remove from the heat. Add the onions and place a small plate on top of the onions to keep them fully submerged in the liquid. Tightly wrap the entire saucepan in aluminum foil to allow the onions to steam. Set the saucepan

aside and allow the onions to come to room temperature. Pour into a nonreactive container and store, covered and refrigerated, for up to 1 week.

PICKLED JAPANESE EGGPLANT

SERVES 6

3 large Japanese eggplants
2 cups vegetable oil
2 cups water
1 cup soy sauce
1 cup rice wine vinegar
  (see Note above)
¼ cup sugar
1 tablespoon hon dashi (pow-
  dered fish stock) (see Note)

1. Trim the eggplants and cut them in half lengthwise.

2. Heat the oil in a large sauté pan over medium heat. Add the eggplants and fry, turning frequently, for about 5 minutes or until golden. Remove from the oil and place on paper towel to drain, patting off any excess oil. Place the eggplant in a shallow, nonreactive storage container. Set aside.

3. Combine the water, soy sauce, vinegar, sugar, and hon dashi in a medium saucepan over medium heat. Bring to a boil; lower the heat and simmer for 10 minutes. Remove from the heat and pour the hot marinade over the eggplant. Set aside to cool. When cool, cover and

refrigerate until ready to use. The eggplant will keep, covered and refrigerated, for up to 1 month.

NOTE: Hon dashi is available at Asian markets.

CURED LEMONS OR LEMON CONFIT

MAKES ABOUT ½ CUP

3 large lemons, preferably
  organic, well washed
1¼ cups sugar
½ cup coarse salt
½ cup cold water
2 tablespoons dry white wine

1. Using a vegetable peeler, remove the rind from the lemons in very thin strips, working from the top to the bottom. Trim the strips of any white pith.

2. Combine the lemon rind with 1 cup of the sugar and the salt in a small nonreactive container. Cover and set aside to cure, stirring occasionally, for 2 hours.

3. Using a small, sharp knife, peel all of the white pith from the zested lemons and remove the lemon segments from the membrane, discarding the pith and membrane. Dice the lemon segments and place them into a small bowl. Cover and set aside.

4. Bring a small pot of water to boil over high heat. Uncover the cured rind and remove it from the container. Brush off any of the sugar-salt mixture that clings to it. Place the rind in the boiling water and boil for 1 minute. Drain well and then repeat the process three times to remove any bitterness. Drain well and pat dry. Cut the cured rind into a fine julienne.

5. Combine the julienned rind with the water and wine and the reserved diced lemon and remaining sugar in a small nonreactive saucepan over medium heat. Bring to a boil. Lower the heat and gently simmer for about 10 minutes or until the mixture is the consistency of marmalade. Remove from the heat and place in a nonreactive container with a lid. Cover and refrigerate for up to 1 month.

Roasted Red Peppers

Red bell peppers, well washed and dried (see Note)
Olive oil
Coarse salt and freshly ground pepper to taste

1. Preheat the oven to 375°F.

2. Cut the peppers in half, lengthwise. Remove the core, membrane, and seeds. Place the peppers in a mixing bowl and toss with enough olive oil to lightly coat. Season to taste with salt and pepper.

3. Place the peppers, cut side down, on a cookie sheet in the preheated oven and bake for about 25 minutes or until the skin is blistered and well colored and the peppers are tender.

4. Place the hot peppers in a resealable plastic bag and seal. Allow to rest for about 15 minutes or until the steam has loosened the skin and the peppers have become cool enough to handle.

5. Unseal the bag and, using your fingertips, push the skin from the peppers. Use immediately or, if using within a day, place the peppers in a nonreactive container and refrigerate until ready to use (see Note).

NOTE: You can prepare any number of peppers at one time. The amount you make should depend on how often you use them.

For longer storage, toss the roasted peppers in olive oil and a bit of balsamic vinegar and season to taste with salt and pepper. Tightly cover and refrigerate for up to 10 days.

Oven-Dried Tomatoes

Ripe plum tomatoes, well washed and dried (see Note)
Olive oil
Coarse salt and freshly ground pepper to taste

1. Preheat the oven to 150°F (or the lowest setting on your oven as long as it is no higher than 200°F).

2. Cut off and discard the stem end of the tomatoes. Cut the tomatoes in half lengthwise. Place the tomatoes in a mixing bowl and toss with enough olive oil to lightly coat. Season to taste with salt and pepper.

3. Place the tomato halves on a cookie sheet in the preheated oven and bake for about 8 hours or until the moisture has evaporated and the tomatoes are soft yet pliable and intensely flavored. Remove from the oven and allow to cool. When cool, place in a resealable plastic bag. Seal and refrigerate for up to 4 weeks.

NOTE: At Tribeca Grill, the pilot light in our ovens emits just enough heat to dry sliced tomatoes overnight. We put in trays just before we close down for the night and by the next morning we have perfectly dried tomatoes. The trick is to use the least amount of constant heat to draw out the moisture over a concentrated period of time. Depending on the oven heat, this can sometimes take up to 12 hours, so don't rush the process!

Spiced Walnuts

Makes ¹/₄ pound

¼ pound walnut halves
¼ cup molasses
1 teaspoon cayenne pepper
1 teaspoon paprika
¼ teaspoon ground cumin
¼ teaspoon freshly ground
   pepper

1. Preheat the oven to 200°F.

2. Place the walnuts in a saucepan of boiling salted water over high heat and return the water to a boil. Immediately drain well and pat the walnuts dry.

3. Place the dried walnuts on a cookie sheet in the preheated oven and roast for about 20 minutes or until the nuts have dried slightly. Remove the nuts from the oven but do not turn off the heat.

4. Combine the molasses with the cayenne, paprika, cumin, and pepper in a mixing bowl. Add the hot nuts and toss to coat well. Spread the coated nuts out on the cookie sheet and return to the hot oven. Bake, turning occasionally, for about 25 minutes or until the nuts are nicely glazed and no longer sticky. Remove the nuts from the oven and allow them to cool. Store, tightly covered, for up to 1 month.

MEATS

Duck Confit

Serves 6

6 duck legs, including the
   thighs
6 shallots, peeled and sliced
5 garlic cloves, peeled and
   sliced
2 bunches of parsley, well
   washed and chopped
4 bay leaves
Pinch of dried thyme
3 tablespoons coarse salt
Approximately 1 pound lard,
   optional

1. Using a boning knife, trim excess fat from the duck legs, reserving the fat.

2. Place the duck fat in a medium sauté pan over low heat and cook for 15 minutes or until all of the fat has been rendered out. Strain the fat into a small bowl, discarding the solids. Cover and reserve. It is not necessary to refrigerate.

3. Combine the shallots, garlic, and parsley in a small bowl. Crumble the bay leaves into the mixture and stir in the thyme.

4. Sprinkle one half of the shallot mixture on the bottom of a large, shallow, nonreactive pan. Sprinkle one half of the salt on top of the shallot mixture. Lay the duck legs on top, skin side up.

5. Sprinkle the remaining salt and then the remaining shallot mixture on top of the duck legs. Cover the entire pan with plastic wrap. Place a heavy pan or cutting board on top and weight it down. Place in the refrigerator to marinate for 5 days.

6. Preheat the oven to 300°F.

7. Remove the legs from the seasoning mixture and brush off any material that clings to them. Place the legs in a small roasting pan with enough rendered fat (and/or lard) to cover. Place in the preheated oven and bake for about 2 hours or until the meat is falling off the bones. Remove from the heat and allow the meat to cool in the fat. Transfer to a ceramic bowl or terrine. Cover and refrigerate for at least 1 week before serving. A completely fat-covered confit will keep, refrigerated, for about 6 months.

NOTE: It is a good idea to start with 3 whole ducks and use the breasts for a main course such as Barbecued Breast of Duck with Peanut-Whipped Potatoes (see page 183) and the bones for stock. If you trim all of the excess fat from the whole ducks, you will be assured of having sufficient fat to cover the confit and will not have to use lard.

Mom's Meatballs

Makes 24 meatballs

2 pounds lean ground beef
2 large eggs
2 medium cloves garlic, minced
1 cup bread crumbs
¾ cup cool water
¼ cup freshly grated Parmesan cheese
¼ cup chopped flat-leaf parsley leaves
1 teaspoon salt
½ teaspoon freshly ground pepper
½ cup vegetable oil

"One year, Joe Pesci asked us to arrange a party for his mother's seventieth birthday, but he had one request: 'It has to be an authentic Italian menu.' I suggested stuffed artichokes, Italian meatballs, and braciole (rolled pork roast), which he loved. However, the menu did give me one problem—I knew that I could never come close to making meatballs the way my mom had done every Sunday when I was growing up. So, I simply called and asked her to help. She was, of course, delighted to have me need her in the kitchen.

"On the day of the party, I drove my mom to the restaurant, gave her an apron, and put her to work. To start the meatballs, I plopped twenty-five pounds of ground beef on the table in front of her. She looked at the meat, then up at me, and with a look of great confusion said, 'What am I supposed to do with that?' 'Make meatballs,' I said. 'But,' she replied, 'I only know how to season two pounds of meat at a time.' So, I divided the meat into twelve different batches and lined them up in front of her. She confidently seasoned each batch individually, and made the best meatballs ever. Mrs. Pesci loved them as much as I do!"

1. Using your hands, combine the meat, eggs, garlic, bread crumbs, water, cheese, parsley, salt, and pepper in a large mixing bowl until just blended. Do not overmix or the meatballs will be tough. (If the mixture feels dry to the touch, add water, a tablespoonful at a time, to make a moist mixture. Only my mom knows what "too dry" and "just moist enough" really mean, so do the best you can. But she does offer this advice: "If you press your finger into the meatball and it makes an easy indentation, the meatballs are perfect.")

2. Roll the meatball mixture into 2-inch round balls.

3. Preheat the oven to low.

4. Line a baking sheet with parchment paper. Set aside.

5. Heat about 2 tablespoons of the oil in a large cast iron (or other heavy-bottomed) skillet over medium heat until very hot but not smoking. Add the meatballs, without crowding the pan, and cook, turning frequently, for about 3 minutes or until nicely browned all over. Lower the heat and con-

tinue cooking, turning frequently, for about 8 minutes or until the meatballs are thoroughly cooked. Place the cooked meatballs on the prepared baking sheet in the preheated oven to keep warm while you continue adding oil to the pan and frying until all the meatballs are cooked. Serve warm.

NOTE: My mom usually serves these meatballs without spaghetti and sauce. However, if spaghetti and meatballs is on your menu, here's a tip from Mom: "When you are going to put the meatballs into your favorite red sauce, fry them quickly over high heat just to brown the outsides—you want them to be raw inside so that they can continue to cook and flavor the sauce without getting dry in the center."

BRAISED OXTAILS

MAKES ABOUT 6 CUPS

2½ pounds oxtail, cut into pieces
1 cup Wondra flour (see Note, page 69)
Coarse salt and freshly ground pepper to taste
2 tablespoons vegetable oil
½ cup port wine
8 cloves garlic, peeled
2 stalks celery, well washed and chopped
1 large carrot, peeled and chopped
1 large onion, peeled and chopped

10 peppercorns
5 fresh thyme sprigs
1 bay leaf
Juice and zest of 1 orange
Approximately 8 cups Veal Stock (or 4 cups each of canned beef and chicken broth) (see page 230)

1. Place the oxtail pieces in a mixing bowl. Add the flour and salt and pepper to taste. Toss to coat the oxtail well.

2. Heat the oil in a Dutch oven over medium-high heat. Add the oxtail and sauté for about 10 minutes or until the oxtail is nicely browned. Add the wine and, using a wooden spoon, stir to lift all of the particles stuck to the bottom of the pan.

3. Preheat the oven to 400°F.

4. Add the garlic, celery, carrot, onion, peppercorns, thyme, and bay leaf to the pan, tossing to combine. Stir in the orange juice and zest and enough stock (or broth) to cover the meat completely. Cover and place in the preheated oven and bake for about 2½ hours or until the meat is almost falling off the bone.

5. Using a slotted spoon, lift the oxtail from the stock. Strain the stock through a fine sieve into a storage container. Shred the meat from the oxtails and place it into the stock. Cover and store, refrigerated, for up to 5 days or freeze for up to 3 months.

DOUGH

PASTA DOUGH

MAKES ABOUT 1 POUND

2 cups all-purpose flour
2 cups semolina flour
1 teaspoon coarse salt
5 large eggs, at room temperature
1 tablespoon olive oil

1. Place the flours and salt in a mound on a clean, flat work surface. Make a well in the center of the mound.

2. One at a time, break the eggs into the well. Add the oil and, using a kitchen fork, beat the eggs and oil lightly. Gradually work the egg mixture into the flour until a loose ball of dough forms. Transfer the dough to a lightly floured surface.

3. Knead the dough for about 5 minutes or until it is soft, smooth, and elastic. Form the dough into a flat disk and cover lightly with plastic wrap. Set aside to rest for 30 minutes.

4. Cut the dough into 4 equal portions and, using a pasta machine, flatten the dough into thin pieces according to the manufacturer's directions. Cut the dough into the shape or size required for a specific recipe.

NOTE: For saffron-flavored pasta, add 1 teaspoon ground saffron threads to the flour and salt.

A WORD ABOUT WINE

DAVID GORDON, the sommelier at Tribeca Grill, has arranged our wine list by style and grape varietal much as a wine enthusiast might do at home. Since customers usually order wine by style (i.e., light and crisp or full and rich), the list is organized in a user-friendly way to assist the diners in easily pairing great wine with their meal.

The Tribeca Grill wine list is international in scope, with a primary focus on American wines. We specifically specialize in Zinfandel, an American grape varietal grown primarily in California. The list features over fifty different bottlings, which makes it the largest Zinfandel collection in New York City. These wines, often produced from old, low-yielding vines, have the concentrated character necessary to complement highly flavored cuisine.

We also feature several vertical listings of California Cabernet Sauvignon that have come directly from the winery libraries to the Tribeca Grill temperature-controlled cellar.

In addition, we have many listings of highly allocated wines (such as Coche Dury Corton Charlemagne, Comte Lafon Meursault Clos de la Barre, Marcassin Chardonnay, Harlan Estate, Bryant Family and Grace Family Cabernet Sauvignon), which we frequently offer at below-market prices. Plus, as a tip of the hat to the restaurant's inaugural year, 1990, we feature a number of French, Italian, and American wines from that outstanding vintage.

The Tribeca Grill continues to host exciting wine dinners and events. Some of the most exciting have been the only New York tasting of ZAP (Zinfandel Advocates and Producers), a Pinot Noir celebration with some of Oregon's and Burgundy's best producers and the first United States visit of the Barolo Boys, a group of Piedmontese wine producers who presented Tribeca Grill with their superb 1990 vintage.

All of our wines, with the exception of those highly allocated bottles, are readily available. Pairing wine with food is a marvelous way to create relaxed, friendly social occasions. Wine dinners at home, with cooks and wine enthusiasts sharing the experience, are some of the best ways we know to entertain and learn, firsthand, about new cuisines and fine wines.

DESSERT WINES

More and more diners are choosing to end their meal with a dessert wine. For fruit-based desserts, we recommend Bonny Doon's Muscat Vin de Glaciere, a California-style ice wine made from the floral Muscat grape. Bursting with the essence of ripe apricot and peach, this concentrated, sweet dessert wine can also be enjoyed on its own.

For chocolate desserts, which can be difficult to pair with wine, a ruby port such as Graham's Six Grapes or Smith Woodhouse Late Bottled Vintage would be a good choice.

Desserts with a nutty component will be complemented by a Tojaki Aszu "5 Puttonyos" from Hungary or a fine-quality Sauternes. These wines have the necessary honey-nut character to accent the flavor of the dessert.

SOURCES

SPICES, CONDIMENTS, AND ASIAN PRODUCTS

Sultan's Delight
POB 090302
Brooklyn, NY 11209
(718) 745-6844

Adriana's Caravan
404 Vanderbilt Street
Brooklyn, NY 11218
(800) 316-0820
www.adriana'scaravan.com

Kalustyan Orient Export
Trading Corporation
123 Lexington Avenue
New York, NY 10016
(212) 685-3451

The Oriental Pantry
423 Great Road
Aston, MA 01720
(800) 828-0368
www.orientalpantry.com

Penzey's Spice House
POB 14348
Waukesha, WI 53187
(414) 574-0278
www.penzeys.com

FOIE GRAS, GAME, AND SPECIALTY MEATS

D'Artagnan
399-419 Saint Paul Avenue
Jersey City, NJ 07306
(800) DARTAGNAN
(201) 792-0748

FISH AND SHELLFISH

Browne Trading Corporation
260 Commercial Street
Portland, ME 04101
(800) 944-9848
www.browne-trading.com

SPECIALTY FOODS, CHEESE, AND GOURMET GROCERIES

Balducci's
(meat and game also)
424 Avenue of the Americas
New York, NY 10011
(212) 673-2600
(800) 225-3822
www.balducci.com

Dean & Deluca
(meat and game also)
560 Broadway
New York, NY 10012
(800) 221-7714
www.dean-deluca.com

Zabar's
2245 Broadway
New York, NY 10024
(212) 787-2000

SPECIALTY KITCHEN-WARE AND APPLIANCES

Bridge Kitchenware
214 East 52nd Street
New York, NY 10022
(212) 688-4220
(212) 758-5387, fax

J. B. Prince Company Inc.
36 East 31st Street
New York, NY 10016
(212) 683-3553
(212) 683-4488, fax

Sommelier David Gordon and general manager Martin Shapiro

INDEX

ABOUT THE AUTHORS

DON PINTABONA is one of the pioneers of contemporary American cuisine. During the past two decades, he has traveled throughout more than 30 countries and worked alongside some of the world's finest chefs. Pinatabona's formal education began at the Culinary Institute of America, where he received an A.O.S. degree in 1982. He went on to work with chefs Daniel Boulud, Charlie Palmer, and Georges Blanc. For the past ten years, Pintabona has been the executive chef of the award-winning Tribeca Grill in New York City. He lives in Brooklyn, New York, with his wife, Christine, and two children, Alex and Daniela.

JUDITH CHOATE, who assisted Don Pintabona with the writing of this book, is an award-winning writer, chef, and pioneer in the promotion of American foods. A member of Women Chefs and Restaurateurs, she is the author of sixteen books and the co-author of many more.